Bryn Mawr Latin Commentaries

Ovid
Fasti II

John F. Miller

Thomas Library
Bryn Mawr College
Bryn Mawr, Pennsylvania

Copyright ©1985 by **Bryn Mawr Commentaries**

Manufactured in the United States of America
ISBN 0-929524-46-2
Printed and distributed by

Bryn Mawr Commentaries
Thomas Library
Bryn Mawr College
Bryn Mawr, PA 19010

Bryn Mawr Latin Commentaries

Editors

Julia Haig Gaisser
Bryn Mawr College

James J. O'Donnell
University of Pennsylvania

The purpose of the Bryn Mawr Latin Commentaries is to make a wide range of classical and post-classical authors accessible to the intermediate student. Each commentary provides the minimum grammatical and lexical information necessary for a first reading of the text.

Introduction

This is an elementary commentary to Book II of Ovid's poetic calendar, the *Fasti*. Its primary aim is to facilitate understanding of the grammar and content of the text. From time to time I have also given brief attention to basic figures of speech and aspects of Ovid's style in the hope that such remarks will stimulate or assist literary interpretation. For the *Fasti* is not simply a sourcebook of Roman religion, as it is often read, but an ambitious poem of considerable artistry which develops many of the themes found throughout Augustan literature in a characteristically Ovidian fashion.

Ovid wrote the *Fasti* in his mid 40s, after he had completed the *Amores, Heroides, Ars amatoria* and *Remedia amoris* and at about the same time that he was composing the *Metamorphoses*. At this time he was the most prominent living Roman poet. From a passage in his *Tristia* (2.549-52) we learn that the work was originally dedicated to Augustus, but after the emperor's death in 14 A.D. Ovid addressed the *Fasti* to Germanicus, the nephew and adopted son of the new emperor Tiberius. Most scholars think that the first dedication was moved to the opening of Book II. Ovid planned a poem of twelve books, one for each month of the year, and may have completed at least a draft of the whole work. But his progress on the poem, as he says in the same lines of the *Tristia*, was interrupted by his exile, and only the first six books (January through June), partially revised during his exile, survive. In 8 A.D. Augustus banished Ovid to the remote town of Tomis on the Black Sea for reasons still not fully understood. Ovid himself attributes the exile to a *carmen* and an *error*. The *carmen* was his *Ars amatoria;* what the indiscretion or *error* was, which Ovid insists was not a crime, we can only guess. He remained at Tomis until his death in or around 17 A.D.

The word *fasti* means "calendar," specifically the official calendar which guided the religious, political and legal activities of the

Roman citizen. Ovid's *Fasti* is a didactic poem--or rather collection of poems--on the religious festivals, historical and other events actually or likely to have been recorded on the civil calendar, together with astronomical and meteorological details of the sort found in farmers' almanacs (*menologia rustica*). Proceeding day by day through the year as recently revised by Julius Caesar, Ovid takes all these topics as points of departure for pseudo-scholarly discussions, ritual directions, panegyrics of Augustus and his family, hymns, and lively narratives.

The headings of the "entries" in our edition reflect the notations on the official *fasti*. After the arabic numeral noting the day of the month according to our modern calendar occurs a capital letter from *A* to *H*. These eight letters, which recur in a cycle throughout the year, are the nundinal letters, so called from the *nundinae* or "market day" held every eight days. (The Romans did not have a week with named days.) The letter designating the market days was determined at the start of the year.

Some days have an abbreviation for the name of the day or its festival after the nundinal letter. Three named days occur every month, all plural in form, the Kalends (*Kalendae*, abbreviated *K* + the adjectival form of the name of the month), the Nones (*Nonae*, = *NON*), and the Ides (*Idus*, = *EID*). Romans dated days of the month by counting backwards from these days, all of which occured at fixed points. See further the commentary on lines 57, 121, and 193.

Finally, every day is marked in the calendars by a letter or letters denoting the character of the day, i.e., whether legal or other business was allowed. Days marked *C* were *dies comitiales*, days when the assemblies of Roman citizens or *comitia* could meet to vote on legislation or elect magistrates or deliver verdicts in some kinds of criminal trials. *F* stood for *dies fastus*, a day on which it was permitted (*fas*) to initiate a civil law suit in the urban praetor's court. *N* represented *dies nefastus*, a day on which the activities allowed on *dies fasti* and *comitiales* were forbidden (*nefas*). *EN* was an abbreviation for *dies endotercissus* (an archaic form of *intercissus*, "cut, split"), a day *nefastus* in the morning and evening when sacrifices were prepared and offered, but *fastus* in the intervening period. The meaning of *NP* is uncertain; perhaps the most plausible explanation is *dies nefastus publicus*, a day on which a religious festival was held on behalf of the people as a whole. Such days had the same restrictions as *dies nefasti*, but were also public holidays, days of rest for both free men and slaves. *FP* has not been convincingly explained, although scholars agree that the *F* stands for *fastus*.

Supplementary Reading

The standard commentary on Ovid's *Fasti* is that of F. Bömer (Heidelberg, 1957-58). J. G. Frazer's five-volume edition (London, 1929) is particularly useful on matters of Roman and comparative religion. The old school editions of the *Fasti* by H. Peter (Leipzig and Berlin; 4th ed. 1907) and G. H. Hallam (bowdlerized; N.Y. and London, 1886) also contain much of value, as does H. Le Bonniec's more recent commentary on Book II (Paris, 1969). The text of Book II accompanying the present commentary is that of J. G. Frazer in the Loeb Classical Library edition (London: William Heinemann Ltd. and Cambridge, Massachusetts: Harvard University Press, 1931).[1]

On the calendar and Roman religion, see also:

W. Warde Fowler, *The Roman Festivals of the Period of the Republic.* London, 1889.
Agnes K. Michels, *The Calendar of the Roman Republic.* Princeton, 1967.
R. M. Ogilvie, *The Romans and their Gods in the Age of Augustus.* New York and London, 1969.
H. H. Scullard, *Festivals and Ceremonies of the Roman Republic.* Ithaca, N.Y., 1981.

---

[1] For an apparatus criticus one should consult Bömer and the new Teubner edition (along with its Appendix) of E.H. Alton, D.E.W. Wormell and E. Courtney (Leipzig, second edition, 1985). The text was produced from a (corrected) computer tape prepared by Theodore Brunner. I have made some changes in punctuation and orthography, and have altered Frazer's text at six places (lines 282, 572, 575, 638, 757, 829) where it seemed to me that other readings were correct.

For literary interpretation:
  John Barsby, *Ovid*. Greece and Rome New Surveys in the Classics No. 12. Oxford, 1978. Chapter 5.
  Elaine Fantham, "Sexual Comedy in Ovid's *Fasti*: Sources and Motivation," *Harvard Studies in Classical Philology* 87 (1983) 185-216.
  Hermann Fränkel, *Ovid: A Poet between Two Worlds*. Berkeley, 1945.
  Stephen Hinds, *The Metamorphosis of Persephone. Ovid and the Self-conscious Muse*. Cambridge, 1987.
  W. R. Johnson, "The Desolation of the *Fasti*," *The Classical Journal* 74 (1979) 7-18.
  A. G. Lee, "Ovid's 'Lucretia'," *Greece and Rome* 22 (1953) 107-118.
  R. J. Littlewood, "Ovid's Lupercalia (*Fasti* 2.267-452): a Study in the Artistry of the *Fasti*," *Latomus* 34 (1975) 1060-72.
  J.C. McKeown, "*Fabula proposito nulla tegenda meo*. Ovid's *Fasti* and Augustan politics," in *Poetry and Politics in the age of Augustus*, edd. T. Woodman and D. West (Cambridge, 1984) 169-87.
  J. F. Miller, "Callimachus and the Augustan Aetiological Elegy," *Aufstieg und Niedergang der römischen Welt* II.30.1 (1982) 371-417.
  Gordon Williams, *Change and Decline: Roman Literature in the Early Empire*. Berkeley, Los Angeles and London, 1978. Chapter 2, "Ovid: the Poet and Politics."
  L. P. Wilkinson, *Ovid Recalled*. Cambridge, 1955. Chapter 8.

Metrical Introduction

Quantitative meter is based on various patterns of long and short syllables. The number of syllables in each word depends on the number of vowels and diphthongs (two vowels pronounced as one--e.g., *ae*). Words are divided into syllables according to the following rules:

1. If a vowel or diphthong is followed by a single consonant, that consonant is taken with the next syllable, and the first syllable is called *open* (e.g., *o-cu-li* has three open syllables).

2. If the vowel or diphthong is followed by two or more consonants, division takes place between the consonants, and the syllable is *closed* (e.g., in *in-tem-pes-ti-vi* the first three syllables are closed, the last two open).

EXCEPTION: If the first consonant is a mute (*b, p, d, t, g,* or *c*) and the second consonant a liquid (*l* or *r*) or a nasal (*m* or *n*), division may be made either before the first consonant (in which case the syllable is open) or after it (in which case the syllable is closed), e.g.: *pa-tri* or *pat-ri*.

NOTE: *x* (= *cs*) and *z* (= *ds*) count as two consonants and *qu* as one; *h* is not considered a consonant and has no power to close a syllable.

The same rules apply at the end of a word, e.g.:

qui-quon-dam-stu-di-o
e-ra-t il-le (note that the second vowel is open)

If a word ending with a vowel or *m* is followed by a word beginning with a vowel or *h*, the first of the adjacent syllables is suppressed (elision), e.g.: *multum ille et* = *mult_ill_et*. But if the second word is *es* or *est* the process is reversed (prodelision), e.g.:

>   *illa est* = *illa_st*
>   *quantum est* = *quantum_st*

>   A syllable is long if:
>   1. it contains a long vowel or diphthong;
>   2. it is closed.

The last syllable in a verse may be either long or short, but by convention is usually counted and marked as long.

>   **Sigla:**
>   ᴗ short
>   — long
>   x anceps (short or long)
>   ⸚ *either* one long syllable *or* two short

In the *Fasti* Ovid uses the elegiac couplet. The first line of the couplet is dactylic hexameter, comprised of six metra or feet, which may be either dactyls (— ᴗ ᴗ) or spondees (— —). The sixth (last) metron or foot is always a spondee; the fifth is generally a dactyl. Word break regularly occurs at one or more fixed points in the line. Word division coinciding with a break between feet or metra is called a *diaeresis* (‖); a division not coinciding with a metrical break is called a *caesura* (^).

Line 1 is analyzed (or "scanned") thus:

>   — ᴗ ᴗ — — — — — ᴗ ᴗ ‖ — ᴗ ᴗ — —
>   Ianus habet finem.^ cum carmine crescit et annus

In this line there is a caesura after the first long of the third foot (masculine caesura) and diaeresis between the fourth and fifth feet (bucolic diaeresis). The line-segments between caesurae or diaereseis are called *cola* ("limbs"). Some cola of this kind are used as independent metrical units. Thus, the colon ending with the masculine caesura is called a *hemiepes:*
>   ⸚ — ⸚ —

The second line of the elegiac couplet (called the pentameter) contains two hemiepes separated by diaeresis. No spondees are allowed in the second hemiepes. Line 2 is scanned:

— ᴗ ᴗ —   — — ‖ — ᴗ ᴗ — ᴗ ᴗ —
alter ut hic mensis sic liber alter eat

For a general survey of Latin metrics, see T.G. Rosenmeyer, Martin Ostwald, and James Halporn, *The Meters of Greek and Latin Poetry* (2nd ed., Norman: University of Oklahoma Press, 1980).

Abbreviations

<   is from.

AG   *Allen and Greenough's New Latin Grammar* (New York, 1975).

Bömer   Franz Bömer, ed. and trans. with commentary, P. Ovidius Naso, *Die Fasten*, 2 vols. (Heidelberg, 1957-58)

cf.   compare; consult (refers to passages in the text).

Frazer Sir James George Frazer, ed. and trans., Ovid's *Fasti* (London and Cambridge, Massachusetts, 1931).

Hallam G. H. Hallam, ed. with commentary, *The Fasti of Ovid* (London and New York, 1886).

L & S Charlton T. Lewis and Charles Short, *A Latin Dictionary* (Oxford, 1969; reprint of 1879 edition).

lit.   literally

OCD   *Oxford Classical Dictionary*, edd. N.G.L. Hammond and H.H. Scullard (Oxford, 1970; 2nd edition).

OLD   *Oxford Latin Dictionary*, ed. P. G. W. Glare (Oxford, 1982).

Peter   Hermann Peter, ed. with commentary, *P. Ovidi Nasonis Fastorum Libri Sex* (Leipzig and Berlin, 1907; 4th rev. ed.).

sc.   *scilicet*; i.e., "understand."

s.v.   *sub voce;* i.e., "under the entry for."

FASTORUM
LIBER SECUNDUS

Ianus habet finem. cum carmine crescit et annus:
  alter ut hic mensis, sic liber alter eat.
nunc primum velis, elegi, maioribus itis:
  exiguum, memini, nuper eratis opus.
ipse ego vos habui faciles in amore ministros, 5
  cum lusit numeris prima iuventa suis,
idem sacra cano signataque tempora fastis:
  ecquis ad haec illinc crederet esse viam?
haec mea militia est: ferimus quae possumus arma,
  dextraque non omni munere nostra vacat. 10
si mihi non valido torquentur pila lacerto,
  nec bellatoris terga premuntur equi,
nec galea tegimur nec acuto cingimur ense,
  (his habilis telis quilibet esse potest),
at tua prosequimur studioso pectore, Caesar, 15
  nomina, per titulos ingredimurque tuos.
ergo ades et placido paulum mea munera voltu
  respice, pacando si quid ab hoste vacas.

februa Romani dixere piamina patres:
  nunc quoque dant verbo plurima signa fidem. 20
pontifices ab rege petunt et flamine lanas,
  quis veterum lingua februa nomen erat,
quaeque capit lictor domibus purgamina versis,
  torrida cum mica farra, vocantur idem;
nomen idem ramo, qui caesus ab arbore pura 25
  casta sacerdotum tempora fronde tegit.
ipse ego flaminicam poscentem februa vidi;
  februa poscenti pinea virga data est.
denique quodcumque est quo corpora nostra piantur,
  hoc apud intonsos nomen habebat avos. 30
mensis ab his dictus, secta quia pelle Luperci
  omne solum lustrant idque piamen habent,
aut quia placatis sunt tempora pura sepulcris,
  tunc cum ferales praeteriere dies.

omne nefas omnemque mali purgamina causam 35
   credebant nostri tollere posse senes.
Graecia principium moris dedit: illa nocentis
   impia lustratos ponere facta putat.
Actoriden Peleus, ipsum quoque Pelea Phoci
   caede per Haemonias solvit Acastus aquas; 40
vectam frenatis per inane draconibus Aegeus
   credulus inmerita Phasida fovit ope;
Amphiareiades Naupactoo Acheloo
   "solve nefas" dixit, solvit et ille nefas.
a! nimium faciles, qui tristia crimina caedis 45
   fluminea tolli posse putatis aqua!

sed tamen (antiqui ne nescius ordinis erres)
   primus, ut est, Iani mensis et ante fuit;
qui sequitur Ianum, veteris fuit ultimus anni:
   tu quoque sacrorum, Termine, finis eras. 50
primus enim Iani mensis, quia ianua prima est:
   qui sacer est imis manibus, imus erat.
postmodo creduntur spatio distantia longo
   tempora bis quini continuasse viri.

          1. H K. FEB. N

Principio mensis Phrygiae contermina Matri 55
   Sospita delubris dicitur aucta novis.
nunc ubi sint illis, quaeris, sacrata Kalendis
   templa deae? longa procubuere die.
cetera ne simili caderent labefacta ruina
   cavit sacrati provida cura ducis, 60
sub quo delubris sentitur nulla senectus;
   nec satis est homines, obligat ille deos.
templorum positor, templorum sancte repostor,
   sit superis, opto, mutua cura tui!
dent tibi caelestes, quos tu caelestibus, annos, 65
   proque tua maneant in statione domo!
tunc quoque vicini lucus celebratur Helerni,
   qua petit aequoreas advena Thybris aquas.
ad penetrale Numae Capitolinumque Tonantem
   inque Iovis summa caeditur arce bidens. 70
saepe graves pluvias adopertus nubibus auster

concitat, aut posita sub nive terra latet.

2. A N

Proximus Hesperias Titan abiturus in undas
   gemmea purpureis cum iuga demet equis,
illa nocte aliquis tollens ad sidera voltum 75
   dicet "ubi est hodie quae Lyra fulsit heri?"
dumque Lyram quaeret, medii quoque terga Leonis
   in liquidas subito mersa notabit aquas.

3. B N

Quem modo caelatum stellis Delphina videbas,
   is fugiet visus nocte sequente tuos, 80
seu fuit occultis felix in amoribus index,
   Lesbida cum domino seu tulit ille lyram.
quod mare non novit, quae nescit Ariona tellus?
   carmine currentes ille tenebat aquas.
saepe sequens agnam lupus est a voce retentus, 85
   saepe avidum fugiens restitit agna lupum;
saepe canes leporesque umbra iacuere sub una,
   et stetit in saxo proxima cerva leae,
et sine lite loquax cum Palladis alite cornix
   sedit, et accipitri iuncta columba fuit. 90
Cynthia saepe tuis fertur, vocalis Arion,
   tamquam fraternis obstipuisse modis.
nomen Arionium Siculas impleverat urbes,
   captaque erat lyricis Ausonis ora sonis;
inde domum repetens puppem conscendit Arion, 95
   atque ita quaesitas arte ferebat opes.
forsitan, infelix, ventos undasque timebas;
   at tibi nave tua tutius aequor erat.
namque gubernator destricto constitit ense
   ceteraque armata conscia turba manu. 100
quid tibi cum gladio? dubiam rege, navita, puppem:
   non haec sunt digitis arma tenenda tuis.
ille, metu pavidus, "mortem non deprecor" inquit,
   "sed liceat sumpta pauca referre lyra."
dant veniam ridentque moram. capit ille coronam, 105
   quae possit crines, Phoebe, decere tuos;
induerat Tyrio bis tinctam murice pallam:

reddidit icta suos pollice chorda sonos,
flebilibus numeris veluti canentia dura
    traiectus penna tempora cantat olor. 110
protinus in medias ornatus desilit undas;
    spargitur impulsa caerula puppis aqua.
inde (fide maius) tergo delphina recurvo
    se memorant oneri supposuisse novo;
ille sedens citharamque tenet pretiumque vehendi 115
    cantat et aequoreas carmine mulcet aquas.
di pia facta vident: astris delphina recepit
    Iuppiter et stellas iussit habere novem.

5. D NON. NP

Nunc mihi mille sonos, quoque est memoratus Achilles,
    vellem, Maeonide, pectus inesse tuum, 120
dum canimus sacras alterno pectine Nonas:
    maximus hic fastis accumulatur honos.
deficit ingenium, maioraque viribus urgent:
    haec mihi praecipuo est ore canenda dies.
quid volui demens elegis imponere tantum 125
    ponderis? heroi res erat ista pedis.
sancte pater patriae, tibi plebs, tibi curia nomen
    hoc dedit, hoc dedimus nos tibi nomen, eques.
res tamen ante dedit. sero quoque vera tulisti
    nomina, iam pridem tu pater orbis eras. 130
hoc tu per terras, quod in aethere Iuppiter alto,
    nomen habes: hominum tu pater, ille deum.
Romule, concedes: facit hic tua magna tuendo
    moenia, tu dederas transilienda Remo.
te Tatius parvique Cures Caeninaque sensit: 135
    hoc duce Romanum est solis utrumque latus.
tu breve nescio quid victae telluris habebas:
    quodcumque est alto sub Iove, Caesar habet.
tu rapis, hic castas duce se iubet esse maritas:
    tu recipis luco, reppulit ille nefas. 140
vis tibi grata fuit, florent sub Caesare leges.
    tu domini nomen, principis ille tenet.
te Remus incusat, veniam dedit hostibus ille.
    caelestem fecit te pater, ille patrem.

iam puer Idaeus media tenus eminet alvo 145

et liquidas mixto nectare fundit aquas.
en etiam, siquis Borean horrere solebat,
gaudeat: a Zephyris mollior aura venit.

9. H N

Quintus ab aequoreis nitidum iubar extulit undis
Lucifer, et primi tempora veris erunt. 150
ne fallare tamen, restant tibi frigora, restant,
magnaque discedens signa reliquit hiems.

11. B N

Tertia nox veniat: Custodem protinus Ursae
aspicies geminos exseruisse pedes.
inter hamadryadas iaculatricemque Dianam 155
Callisto sacri pars fuit una chori.
illa deae tangens arcus "quos tangimus arcus,
este meae testes virginitatis" ait.
Cynthia laudavit, "promissa"que "foedera serva,
et comitum princeps tu mihi" dixit "eris." 160
foedera servasset, si non formosa fuisset:
cavit mortales, de Iove crimen habet.
mille feras Phoebe silvis venata redibat
aut plus aut medium sole tenente diem.
ut tetigit lucum (densa niger ilice lucus, 165
in medio gelidae fons erat altus aquae),
"hic" ait "in silva, virgo Tegeaea, lavemur!"
erubuit falso virginis illa sono.
dixerat et nymphis. nymphae velamina ponunt;
hanc pudet et tardae dat mala signa morae. 170
exuerat tunicas; uteri manifesta tumore
proditur indicio ponderis ipsa suo.
cui dea "virgineos, periura Lycaoni, coetus
desere nec castas pollue" dixit "aquas."
luna novum decies implerat cornibus orbem: 175
quae fuerat virgo credita, mater erat.
laesa furit Iuno, formam mutatque puellae.
quid facis? invito est pectore passa Iovem.
utque ferae vidit turpes in paelice voltus,
"huius in amplexus Iuppiter" inquit "eat!" 180
ursa per incultos errabat squalida montes,

quae fuerat summo nuper amata Iovi.
iam tria lustra puer furto conceptus agebat,
cum mater nato est obvia facta suo.
illa quidem, tamquam cognosceret, adstitit amens 185
et gemuit: gemitus verba parentis erant.
hanc puer ignarus iaculo fixisset acuto,
ni foret in superas raptus uterque domos.
signa propinqua micant: prior est, quam dicimus Arcton,
Arctophylax formam terga sequentis habet. 190
saevit adhuc canamque rogat Saturnia Tethyn
Maenaliam tactis ne lavet Arcton aquis.

13. D EID. NP

Idibus agrestis fumant altaria Fauni
hic ubi discretas insula rumpit aquas.
haec fuit illa dies, in qua Veientibus armis 195
ter centum Fabii ter cecidere duo.
una domus vires et onus susceperat Urbis:
sumunt gentiles arma professa manus.
egreditur castris miles generosus ab isdem,
e quis dux fieri quilibet aptus erat. 200
Carmentis portae dextro est via proxima iano:
ire per hanc noli, quisquis es; omen habet.
illa fama refert Fabios exisse trecentos:
porta vacat culpa, sed tamen omen habet.
ut celeri passu Cremeram tetigere rapacem 205
(turbidus hibernis ille fluebat aquis),
castra loco ponunt: destrictis ensibus ipsi
Tyrrhenum valido Marte per agmen eunt,
non aliter quam cum Libyca de gente leones
invadunt sparsos lata per arva greges. 210
diffugiunt hostes inhonestaque volnera tergo
accipiunt: Tusco sanguine terra rubet.
sic iterum, sic saepe cadunt. ubi vincere aperte
non datur, insidias armaque tecta parant.
campus erat, campi claudebant ultima colles 215
silvaque montanas occulere apta feras.
in medio paucos armentaque rara relinquunt,
cetera virgultis abdita turba latet.
ecce velut torrens undis pluvialibus auctus
aut nive, quae Zephyro victa tepente fluit, 220

per sata perque vias fertur nec, ut ante solebat,
    riparum clausas margine finit aquas:
sic Fabii vallem latis discursibus implent,
    quodque vident, sternunt, nec metus alter inest.
quo ruitis, generosa domus? male creditis hosti: 225
    simplex nobilitas, perfida tela cave!
fraude perit virtus: in apertos undique campos
    prosiliunt hostes et latus omne tenent.
quid faciant pauci contra tot milia fortes?
    quidve, quod in misero tempore restet, habent?   230
sicut aper longe silvis Laurentibus actus
    fulmineo celeres dissipat ore canes,
mox tamen ipse perit, sic non moriuntur inulti
    volneraque alterna dantque feruntque manu.
una dies Fabios ad bellum miserat omnes: 235
    ad bellum missos perdidit una dies.
ut tamen Herculeae superessent semina gentis,
    credibile est ipsos consuluisse deos;
nam puer impubes et adhuc non utilis armis
    unus de Fabia gente relictus erat,   240
scilicet ut posses olim tu, Maxime, nasci,
    cui res cunctando restituenda foret.

14. E N

Continuata loco tria sidera, Corvus et Anguis
    et medius Crater inter utrumque iacet.
Idibus illa latent, oriuntur nocte sequenti.   245
    quae, tibi, cur tria sint tam sociata, canam.
forte Iovi Phoebus festum sollemne parabat
    (non faciet longas fabula nostra moras):
"i, mea" dixit "avis, ne quid pia sacra moretur,
    et tenuem vivis fontibus adfer aquam."   250
corvus inauratum pedibus cratera recurvis
    tollit et aerium pervolat altus iter.
stabat adhuc duris ficus densissima pomis:
    temptat eam rostro; non erat apta legi.
inmemor imperii sedisse sub arbore fertur,   255
    dum fierent tarda dulcia poma mora.
iamque satur nigris longum rapit unguibus hydrum
    ad dominumque redit fictaque verba refert:
"hic mihi causa morae, vivarum obsessor aquarum:

hic tenuit fontes officiumque meum." 260
"addis" ait "culpae mendacia," Phoebus "et audes
  fatidicum verbis fallere velle deum?
at tibi, dum lactens haerebit in arbore ficus,
  de nullo gelidae fonte bibentur aquae."
dixit, et antiqui monumenta perennia facti, 265
  Anguis, Avis, Crater sidera iuncta micant.

15. F LUPER. NP

Tertia post Idus nudos aurora Lupercos
  aspicit, et Fauni sacra bicornis eunt.
dicite, Pierides, sacrorum quae sit origo,
  attigerint Latias unde petita domos. 270
Pana deum pecoris veteres coluisse feruntur
  Arcades: Arcadiis plurimus ille iugis.
testis erit Pholoe, testes Stymphalides undae,
  quique citis Ladon in mare currit aquis,
cinctaque pinetis nemoris iuga Nonacrini, 275
  altaque Cyllene Parrhasiaeque nives.
Pan erat armenti, Pan illic numen equarum;
  munus ob incolumes ille ferebat oves.
transtulit Evander silvestria numina secum;
  hic, ubi nunc Urbs est, tum locus urbis erat. 280
inde deum colimus devectaque sacra Pelasgis:
  flamen ad haec prisco more Dialis erat.
cur igitur currant, et cur (sic currere mos est)
  nuda ferant posita corpora veste, rogas?
ipse deus velox discurrere gaudet in altis 285
  montibus et subitas concipit ipse fugas;
ipse deus nudus nudos iubet ire ministros,
  nec satis ad cursus commoda vestis erat.
ante Iovem genitum terras habuisse feruntur
  Arcades, et luna gens prior illa fuit. 290
vita feris similis, nullos agitata per usus:
  artis adhuc expers et rude volgus erat.
pro domibus frondes norant, pro frugibus herbas;
  nectar erat palmis hausta duabus aqua.
nullus anhelabat sub adunco vomere taurus, 295
  nulla sub imperio terra colentis erat:
nullus adhuc erat usus equi; se quisque ferebat:
  ibat ovis lana corpus amicta sua.

Ovid, *Fasti II* 17

sub Iove durabant et corpora nuda gerebant
   docta graves imbres et tolerare Notos. 300
nunc quoque detecti referunt monumenta vetusti
   moris et antiquas testificantur opes.
sed cur praecipue fugiat velamina Faunus,
   traditur antiqui fabula plena ioci.
forte comes dominae iuvenis Tirynthius ibat: 305
   vidit ab excelso Faunus utrumque iugo.
vidit et incaluit, "montana"que "numina," dixit
   "nil mihi vobiscum est: hic meus ardor erit."
ibat odoratis umeros perfusa capillis
   Maeonis aurato conspicienda sinu: 310
aurea pellebant tepidos umbracula soles,
   quae tamen Herculeae sustinuere manus.
iam Bacchi nemus et Tmoli vineta tenebat,
   Hesperos et fusco roscidus ibat equo.
antra subit tofis laqueata et pumice vivo; 315
   garrulus in primo limine rivus erat.
dumque parant epulas potandaque vina ministri,
   cultibus Alciden instruit illa suis.
dat tenuis tunicas Gaetulo murice tinctas,
   dat teretem zonam, qua modo cincta fuit. 320
ventre minor zona est; tunicarum vincla relaxat,
   ut posset magnas exseruisse manus.
fregerat armillas non illa ad bracchia factas,
   scindebant magni vincula parva pedes.
ipsa capit clavamque gravem spoliumque leonis 325
   conditaque in pharetra tela minora sua.
sic epulis functi sic dant sua corpora somno,
   et positis iuxta secubuere toris;
causa, repertori vitis quia sacra parabant,
   quae facerent pure, cum foret orta dies. 330
noctis erat medium. quid non amor improbus audet?
   roscida per tenebras Faunus ad antra venit,
utque videt comites somno vinoque solutos,
   spem capit in dominis esse soporis idem.
intrat, et huc illuc temerarius errat adulter 335
   et praefert cautas subsequiturque manus.
venerat ad strati captata cubilia lecti
   et felix prima sorte futurus erat.
ut tetigit fulvi saetis hirsuta leonis
   vellera, pertimuit sustinuitque manum 340

attonitusque metu rediit, ut saepe viator
  turbatus viso rettulit angue pedem.
inde tori, qui iunctus erat, velamina tangit
  mollia, mendaci decipiturque nota.
ascendit spondaque sibi propiore recumbit, 345
  et tumidum cornu durius inguen erat.
interea tunicas ora subducit ab ima:
  horrebant densis aspera crura pilis.
cetera temptantem subito Tirynthius heros
  reppulit: e summo decidit ille toro. 350
fit sonus, inclamat comites et lumina poscit
  Maeonis: inlatis ignibus acta patent.
ille gemit lecto graviter deiectus ab alto,
  membraque de dura vix sua tollit humo.
ridet et Alcides et qui videre iacentem, 355
  ridet amatorem Lyda puella suum.
veste deus lusus fallentes lumina vestes
  non amat et nudos ad sua sacra vocat.
adde peregrinis causas, mea Musa, Latinas,
  inque suo noster pulvere currat equus. 360
cornipedi Fauno caesa de more capella
  venit ad exiguas turba vocata dapes.
dumque sacerdotes veribus transuta salignis
  exta parant, medias sole tenente vias,
Romulus et frater pastoralisque iuventus 365
  solibus et campo corpora nuda dabant;
caestibus et iaculis et misso pondere saxi
  bracchia per lusus experienda dabant:
pastor ab excelso "per devia rura iuvencos,
  Romule, praedones, et Reme," dixit "agunt." 370
longum erat armari: diversis exit uterque
  partibus; occursu praeda recepta Remi.
ut rediit, veribus stridentia detrahit exta
  atque ait "haec certe non nisi victor edet."
dicta facit, Fabiique simul. venit inritus illuc 375
  Romulus et mensas ossaque nuda videt;
risit et indoluit Fabios potuisse Remumque
  vincere, Quintilios non potuisse suos.
fama manet facti: posito velamine currunt,
  et memorem famam, quod bene cessit, habet. 380

forsitan et quaeras, cur sit locus ille Lupercal,

quaeve diem tali nomine causa notet.
Silvia Vestalis caelestia semina partu
  ediderat, patruo regna tenente suo.
is iubet auferri parvos et in amne necari: 385
  quid facis? ex istis Romulus alter erit.
iussa recusantes peragunt lacrimosa ministri,
  flent tamen et geminos in loca iussa ferunt.
Albula, quem Tiberim mersus Tiberinus in undis
  reddidit, hibernis forte tumebat aquis: 390
hic, ubi nunc fora sunt, lintres errare videres,
  quaque iacent valles, Maxime Circe, tuae.
huc ubi venerunt (neque enim procedere possunt
  longius), ex illis unus et alter ait:
"at quam sunt similes! at quam formosus uterque! 395
  plus tamen ex illis iste vigoris habet.
si genus arguitur voltu, nisi fallit imago,
  nescio quem in vobis suspicor esse deum--
at si quis vestrae deus esset originis auctor,
  in tam praecipiti tempore ferret opem; 400
ferret opem certe, si non ope mater egeret,
  quae facta est uno mater et orba die.
nata simul, moritura simul, simul ite sub undas
  corpora!" desierat deposuitque sinu.
vagierunt ambo pariter: sensisse putares. 405
  hi redeunt udis in sua tecta genis.
sustinet impositos summa cavus alveus unda:
  heu quantum fati parva tabella tulit!
alveus in limo silvis adpulsus opacis
  paulatim fluvio deficiente sedet. 410
arbor erat: remanent vestigia, quaeque vocatur
  Rumina nunc ficus, Romula ficus erat.
venit ad expositos (mirum!) lupa feta gemellos:
  quis credat pueris non nocuisse feram?
non nocuisse parum est, prodest quoque: quos lupa nutrit, 415
  perdere cognatae sustinuere manus.
constitit et cauda teneris blanditur alumnis
  et fingit lingua corpora bina sua.
Marte satos scires: timor afuit, ubera ducunt
  nec sibi promissi lactis aluntur ope. 420
illa loco nomen fecit, locus ipse Lupercis;
  magna dati nutrix praemia lactis habet.
quid vetat Arcadio dictos a monte Lupercos?

Faunus in Arcadia templa Lycaeus habet.

nupta, quid exspectas? non tu pollentibus herbis 425
  nec prece nec magico carmine mater eris;
excipe fecundae patienter verbera dextrae,
  iam socer optatum nomen habebit avi.
nam fuit illa dies, dura cum sorte maritae
  reddebant uteri pignora rara sui. 430
"quid mihi" clamabat "prodest rapuisse Sabinas,"
  Romulus (hoc illo sceptra tenente fuit)
"si mea non vires, sed bellum iniuria fecit?
  utilius fuerat non habuisse nurus."
monte sub Esquilio multis incaeduus annis 435
  Iunonis magnae nomine lucus erat.
huc ubi venerunt, pariter nuptaeque virique
  suppliciter posito procubuere genu,
cum subito motae tremuere cacumina silvae
  et dea per lucos mira locuta suos: 440
"Italidas matres" inquit "sacer hircus inito."
  obstipuit dubio territa turba sono.
augur erat (nomen longis intercidit annis;
  nuper ab Etrusca venerat exul humo),
ille caprum mactat, iussae sua terga puellae 445
  pellibus exsectis percutienda dabant.
luna resumebat decimo nova cornua motu,
  virque pater subito nuptaque mater erat.
gratia Lucinae! dedit haec tibi nomina lucus,
  aut quia principium tu, dea, lucis habes. 450
parce, precor, gravidis, facilis Lucina, puellis
  maturumque utero molliter aufer onus.

orta dies fuerit, tu desine credere ventis:
  perdidit illius temporis aura fidem;
flamina non constant, et sex reserata diebus 455
  carceris Aeolii ianua lata patet.

iam levis obliqua subsedit Aquarius urna:
  proximus aetherios excipe, Piscis, equos.
te memorant fratremque tuum (nam iuncta micatis
  signa) duos tergo sustinuisse deos. 460
terribilem quondam fugiens Typhona Dione,
  tunc cum pro caelo Iuppiter arma tulit,

venit ad Euphraten comitata Cupidine parvo
  inque Palaestinae margine sedit aquae.
populus et cannae riparum summa tenebant, 465
  spemque dabant salices hos quoque posse tegi.
dum latet, insonuit vento nemus; illa timore
  pallet et hostiles credit adesse manus,
utque sinu tenuit natum, "succurrite, nymphae,
  et dis auxilium ferte duobus!" ait. 470
nec mora, prosiluit. pisces subiere gemelli:
  pro quo nunc dignum sidera munus habent.
inde nefas ducunt genus hoc imponere mensis
  nec violant timidi piscibus ora Syri.

16. G EN 17. H QUIR. NP

Proxima lux vacua est, at tertia dicta Quirino: 475
  qui tenet hoc nomen, Romulus ante fuit,
sive quod hasta curis priscis est dicta Sabinis
  (bellicus a telo venit in astra deus),
sive suum regi nomen posuere Quirites,
  seu quia Romanis iunxerat ille Cures. 480
nam pater armipotens, postquam nova moenia vidit
  multaque Romulea bella peracta manu,
"Iuppiter," inquit, "habet Romana potentia vires:
  sanguinis officio non eget illa mei.
redde patri natum. quamvis intercidit alter, 485
  pro se proque Remo, qui mihi restat, erit.
'unus erit, quem tu tolles in caerula caeli'
  tu mihi dixisti: sint rata dicta Iovis."
Iuppiter adnuerat. nutu tremefactus uterque
  est polus, et caeli pondera movit Atlas. 490
est locus, antiqui Capreae dixere paludem:
  forte tuis illic, Romule, iura dabas.
sol fugit, et removent subeuntia nubila caelum,
  et gravis effusis decidit imber aquis.
hinc tonat, hinc missis abrumpitur ignibus aether: 495
  fit fuga, rex patriis astra petebat equis.
luctus erat, falsaeque patres in crimine caedis,
  haesissetque animis forsitan illa fides;
sed Proculus Longa veniebat Iulius Alba,
  lunaque fulgebat, nec facis usus erat, 500
cum subito motu saepes tremuere sinistrae:

rettulit ille gradus, horrueruntque comae.
pulcher et humano maior trabeaque decorus
  Romulus in media visus adesse via
et dixisse simul "prohibe lugere Quirites, 505
  nec violent lacrimis numina nostra suis;
tura ferant placentque novum pia turba Quirinum
  et patrias artes militiamque colant."
iussit et in tenues oculis evanuit auras;
  convocat hic populos iussaque verba refert. 510
templa deo fiunt: collis quoque dictus ab illo est,
  et referunt certi sacra paterna dies.

lux quoque cur eadem Stultorum festa vocetur,
  accipe. parva quidem causa, sed apta, subest.
non habuit doctos tellus antiqua colonos: 515
  lassabant agiles aspera bella viros.
plus erat in gladio quam curvo laudis aratro:
  neglectus domino pauca ferebat ager.
farra tamen veteres iaciebant, farra metebant,
  primitias Cereri farra resecta dabant. 520
usibus admoniti flammis torrenda dederunt
  multaque peccato damna tulere suo.
nam modo verrebant nigras pro farre favillas,
  nunc ipsas ignes corripuere casas.
facta dea est Fornax: laeti Fornace coloni 525
  orant, ut fruges temperet illa suas.
curio legitimis nunc Fornacalia verbis
  maximus indicit nec stata sacra facit,
inque foro, multa circum pendente tabella,
  signatur certa curia quaeque nota; 530
stultaque pars populi, quae sit sua curia, nescit,
  sed facit extrema sacra relata die.

21. D FERAL. F

Est honor et tumulis. animas placate paternas
  parvaque in exstinctas munera ferte pyras.
parva petunt manes: pietas pro divite grata est 535
  munere; non avidos Styx habet ima deos.
tegula porrectis satis est velata coronis
  et sparsae fruges parcaque mica salis
inque mero mollita Ceres violaeque solutae:

haec habeat media testa relicta via. 540
nec maiora veto, sed et his placabilis umbra est:
    adde preces positis et sua verba focis.
hunc morem Aeneas, pietatis idoneus auctor,
    attulit in terras, iuste Latine, tuas;
ille patris genio sollemnia dona ferebat: 545
    hinc populi ritus edidicere pios.
at quondam, dum longa gerunt pugnacibus armis
    bella, Parentales deseruere dies.
non impune fuit; nam dicitur omine ab isto
    Roma suburbanis incaluisse rogis. 550
vix equidem credo: bustis exisse feruntur
    et tacitae questi tempore noctis avi,
perque vias Urbis latosque ululasse per agros
    deformes animas, volgus inane, ferunt.
post ea praeteriti tumulis redduntur honores, 555
    prodigiisque venit funeribusque modus.
dum tamen haec fiunt, viduae cessate puellae:
    exspectet puros pinea taeda dies,
nec tibi, quae cupidae matura videbere matri,
    comat virgineas hasta recurva comas. 560
conde tuas, Hymenaee, faces et ab ignibus atris
    aufer! habent alias maesta sepulcra faces.
di quoque templorum foribus celentur opertis,
    ture vacent arae stentque sine igne foci.
nunc animae tenues et corpora functa sepulcris 565
    errant, nunc posito pascitur umbra cibo.
nec tamen haec ultra, quam tot de mense supersint
    Luciferi, quot habent carmina nostra pedes.
hanc, quia iusta ferunt, dixere Feralia lucem;
    ultima placandis manibus illa dies. 570

ecce anus in mediis residens annosa puellis
    sacra facit Tacitae (vix tamen ipsa tacet),
et digitis tria tura tribus sub limine ponit,
    qua brevis occultum mus sibi fecit iter;
tunc cantata ligat ter fusco licia plumbo 575
    et septem nigras versat in ore fabas,
quodque pice adstrinxit, quod acu traiecit aena,
    obsutum maenae torret in igne caput;
vina quoque instillat: vini quodcumque relictum est,
    aut ipsa aut comites, plus tamen ipsa, bibit. 580

"hostiles linguas inimicaque vinximus ora"
    dicit discedens ebriaque exit anus.
protinus a nobis, quae sit dea Muta, requires:
    disce, per antiquos quae mihi nota senes.
Iuppiter, immodico Iuturnae victus amore,　　　　585
    multa tulit tanto non patienda deo:
illa modo in silvis inter coryleta latebat,
    nunc in cognatas desiliebat aquas.
convocat hic nymphas, Latium quaecumque tenebant,
    et iacit in medio talia verba choro:　　　　590
"invidet ipsa sibi vitatque quod expedit illi
    vestra soror, summo concubuisse deo.
consulite ambobus; nam quae mea magna voluptas,
    utilitas vestrae magna sororis erit.
vos illi in prima fugienti obsistite ripa,　　　　595
    ne sua fluminea corpora mergat aqua."
dixerat; adnuerant nymphae Tiberinides omnes,
    quaeque colunt thalamos, Ilia diva, tuos.
forte fuit nais, Lara nomine, prima sed illi
    dicta bis antiquum syllaba nomen erat,　　　　600
ex vitio positum. saepe illi dixerat Almo
    "nata, tene linguam," nec tamen illa tenet.
quae simul ac tetigit Iuturnae stagna sororis,
    "effuge" ait "ripas"; dicta refertque Iovis.
illa etiam Iunonem adiit, miserataque nuptas　　　　605
    "naida Iuturnam vir tuus" inquit "amat."
Iuppiter intumuit, quaque est non usa modeste,
    eripit huic linguam Mercuriumque vocat:
"duc hanc ad manes: locus ille silentibus aptus.
    nympha, sed infernae nympha paludis erit."　　　　610
iussa Iovis fiunt. accepit lucus euntes:
    dicitur illa duci tunc placuisse deo.
vim parat hic, voltu pro verbis illa precatur,
    et frustra muto nititur ore loqui.
fitque gravis geminosque parit, qui compita servant　　　　615
    et vigilant nostra semper in Urbe, Lares.

22. E C

Proxima cognati dixere Caristia cari,
    et venit ad socios turba propinqua deos.
scilicet a tumulis et, qui periere, propinquis

protinus ad vivos ora referre iuvat 620
postque tot amissos, quicquid de sanguine restat,
  aspicere et generis dinumerare gradus.
innocui veniant: procul hinc, procul impius esto
  frater et in partus mater acerba suos,
cui pater est vivax, qui matris digerit annos, 625
  quae premit invisam socrus iniqua nurum.
Tantalidae fratres absint et Iasonis uxor
  et quae ruricolis semina tosta dedit,
et soror et Procne Tereusque duabus iniquus
  et quicumque suas per scelus auget opes. 630
dis generis date tura boni (Concordia fertur
  illa praecipue mitis adesse die)
et libate dapes, ut, grati pignus honoris,
  nutriat incinctos missa patella Lares.
iamque, ubi suadebit placidos nox humida somnos, 635
  larga precaturi sumite vina manu,
et "bene vos, bene te, patriae pater, optime Caesar!"
  dicite; suffuso sint bona verba mero.

23. F TER. NP

Nox ubi transierit, solito celebretur honore
  separat indicio qui deus arva suo. 640
Termine, sive lapis, sive es defossus in agro
  stipes, ab antiquis tu quoque numen habes.
te duo diversa domini de parte coronant
  binaque serta tibi binaque liba ferunt.
ara fit: huc ignem curto fert rustica testu 645
  sumptum de tepidis ipsa colona focis.
ligna senex minuit concisaque construit arte
  et solida ramos figere pugnat humo;
tum sicco primas inritat cortice flammas,
  stat puer et manibus lata canistra tenet. 650
inde ubi ter fruges medios immisit in ignis,
  porrigit incisos filia parva favos.
vina tenent alii: libantur singula flammis;
  spectant, et linguis candida turba favet.
spargitur et caeso communis Terminus agno 655
  nec queritur, lactans cum sibi porca datur.
conveniunt celebrantque dapes vicinia simplex
  et cantant laudes, Termine sancte, tuas:

tu populos urbesque et regna ingentia finis:
   omnis erit sine te litigiosus ager.   660
nulla tibi ambitio est, nullo corrumperis auro,
   legitima servas credita rura fide.
si tu signasses olim Thyreatida terram,
   corpora non leto missa trecenta forent,
nec foret Othryades congestis lectus in armis.   665
   o quantum patriae sanguinis ille dedit!
quid, nova cum fierent Capitolia? nempe deorum
   cuncta Iovi cessit turba locumque dedit:
Terminus, ut veteres memorant, inventus in aede
   restitit et magno cum Iove templa tenet.   670
nunc quoque, se supra ne quid nisi sidera cernat,
   exiguum templi tecta foramen habent.
Termine, post illud levitas tibi libera non est:
   qua positus fueris in statione, mane;
nec tu vicino quicquam concede roganti,   675
   ne videare hominem praeposuisse Iovi;
et seu vomeribus seu tu pulsabere rastris,
   clamato "tuus est hic ager, ille suus!"
est via, quae populum Laurentes ducit in agros,
   quondam Dardanio regna petita duci: 680
illa lanigeri pecoris tibi, Termine, fibris
   sacra videt fieri sextus ab Urbe lapis.
gentibus est aliis tellus data limite certo:
   Romanae spatium est Urbis et orbis idem.

24. G REGIF. N

Nunc mihi dicenda est regis fuga: traxit ab illa   685
   sextus ab extremo nomina mense dies.
ultima Tarquinius Romanae gentis habebat
   regna, vir iniustus, fortis ad arma tamen.
ceperat hic alias, alias everterat urbes
   et Gabios turpi fecerat arte suos.   690
namque trium minimus, proles manifesta Superbi,
   in medios hostes nocte silente venit.
nudarant gladios: "occidite" dixit "inermem!
   hoc cupiant fratres Tarquiniusque pater,
qui mea crudeli laceravit verbere terga."   695
   dicere ut hoc posset, verbera passus erat.
luna fuit: spectant iuvenem gladiosque recondunt

tergaque, deducta veste, notata vident.
flent quoque et, ut secum tueatur bella, precantur.
callidus ignaris adnuit ille viris.
iamque potens misso genitorem appellat amico,
perdendi Gabios quod sibi monstret iter.
hortus odoratis suberat cultissimus herbis,
sectus humum rivo lene sonantis aquae:
illic Tarquinius mandata latentia nati
accipit et virga lilia summa metit.
nuntius ut rediit decussaque lilia dixit,
filius "agnosco iussa parentis" ait.
nec mora, principibus caesis ex urbe Gabina,
traduntur ducibus moenia nuda suis.
ecce, nefas visu, mediis altaribus anguis
exit et exstinctis ignibus exta rapit.
consulitur Phoebus. sors est ita reddita: "matri
qui dederit princeps oscula, victor erit."
oscula quisque suae matri properata tulerunt,
non intellecto credula turba deo.
Brutus erat stulti sapiens imitator, ut esset
tutus ab insidiis, dire Superbe, tuis.
ille iacens pronus matri dedit oscula Terrae,
creditus offenso procubuisse pede.
cingitur interea Romanis Ardea signis
et patitur longas obsidione moras.
dum vacat et metuunt hostes committere pugnam,
luditur in castris, otia miles agit.
Tarquinius iuvenis socios dapibusque meroque
accipit; ex illis rege creatus ait:
"dum nos sollicitos pigro tenet Ardea bello
nec sinit ad patrios arma referre deos,
ecquid in officio torus est socialis? et ecquid
coniugibus nostris mutua cura sumus?"
quisque suam laudat: studiis certamina crescunt,
et fervet multo linguaque corque mero.
surgit, cui dederat clarum Collatia nomen:
"non opus est verbis, credite rebus!" ait.
"nox superest: tollamur equis Urbemque petamus!"
dicta placent, frenis impediuntur equi;
pertulerant dominos. regalia protinus illi
tecta petunt: custos in fore nullus erat.
ecce nurus regis fusis per colla coronis

inveniunt posito pervigilare mero. 740
inde cito passu petitur Lucretia: nebat,
   ante torum calathi lanaque mollis erat.
lumen ad exiguum famulae data pensa trahebant,
   inter quas tenui sic ait illa sono:
"mittenda est domino (nunc, nunc properate, puellae!) 745
   quam primum nostra facta lacerna manu.
quid tamen auditis? nam plura audire potestis:
   quantum de bello dicitur esse super?
postmodo victa cades: melioribus, Ardea, restas,
   improba, quae nostros cogis abesse viros. 750
sint tantum reduces! sed enim temerarius ille
   est meus et stricto qualibet ense ruit.
mens abit, et morior, quotiens pugnantis imago
   me subit, et gelidum pectora frigus habet."
desinit in lacrimas intentaque fila remittit, 755
   in gremio voltum deposuitque suum.
hoc ipsum decuit: lacrimae decuere pudicam,
   et facies animo dignaque parque fuit.
"pone metum, veni!" coniunx ait. illa revixit
   deque viri collo dulce pependit onus. 760
interea iuvenis furiales regius ignis
   concipit et caeco raptus amore furit.
forma placet niveusque color flavique capilli
   quique aderat nulla factus ab arte decor;
verba placent et vox et quod corrumpere non est; 765
   quoque minor spes est, hoc magis ille cupit.
iam dederat cantus lucis praenuntius ales,
   cum referunt iuvenes in sua castra pedem.
carpitur adtonitos absentis imagine sensus
   ille. recordanti plura magisque placent: 770
"sic sedit, sic culta fuit, sic stamina nevit,
   neglectae collo sic iacuere comae,
hos habuit voltus, haec illi verba fuerunt,
   hic color, haec facies, hic decor oris erat."
ut solet a magno fluctus languescere flatu, 775
   sed tamen a vento, qui fuit, unda tumet,
sic, quamvis aberat placitae praesentia formae,
   quem dederat praesens forma, manebat amor.
ardet et iniusti stimulis agitatus amoris
   comparat indigno vimque dolumque toro. 780
"exitus in dubio est: audebimus ultima!" dixit,

"viderit! audentes forsque deusque iuvat.
cepimus audendo Gabios quoque." talia fatus
ense latus cinxit tergaque pressit equi.
accipit aerata iuvenem Collatia porta, 785
condere iam voltus sole parante suos.
hostis ut hospes init penetralia Collatini:
comiter excipitur; sanguine iunctus erat.
quantum animis erroris inest! parat inscia rerum
infelix epulas hostibus illa suis. 790
functus erat dapibus: poscunt sua tempora somnum;
nox erat et tota lumina nulla domo.
surgit et aurata vagina liberat ensem
et venit in thalamos, nupta pudica, tuos.
utque torum pressit, "ferrum, Lucretia, mecum est. 795
natus" ait "regis Tarquiniusque loquor!"
illa nihil: neque enim vocem viresque loquendi
aut aliquid toto pectore mentis habet;
sed tremit, ut quondam stabulis deprensa relictis
parva sub infesto cum iacet agna lupo. 800
quid faciat? pugnet? vincetur femina pugnans.
clamet? at in dextra, qui vetet, ensis erat.
effugiat? positis urgentur pectora palmis,
tunc primum externa pectora tacta manu.
instat amans hostis precibus pretioque minisque: 805
nec prece nec pretio nec movet ille minis.
"nil agis: eripiam" dixit "per crimina vitam:
falsus adulterii testis adulter ero:
interimam famulum, cum quo deprensa fereris."
succubuit famae victa puella metu. 810
quid, victor, gaudes? haec te victoria perdet.
heu quanto regnis nox stetit una tuis!
iamque erat orta dies: passis sedet illa capillis,
ut solet ad nati mater itura rogum,
grandaevumque patrem fido cum coniuge castris 815
evocat, et posita venit uterque mora.
utque vident habitum, quae luctus causa, requirunt,
cui paret exsequias, quove sit icta malo.
illa diu reticet pudibundaque celat amictu
ora: fluunt lacrimae more perennis aquae. 820
hinc pater, hinc coniunx lacrimas solantur et orant,
indicet, et caeco flentque paventque metu.
ter conata loqui ter destitit, ausaque quarto

non oculos ideo sustulit illa suos.
"hoc quoque Tarquinio debebimus? eloquar," inquit, 825
"eloquar infelix dedecus ipsa meum?"
quaeque potest, narrat. restabant ultima: flevit,
et matronales erubuere genae.
dant veniam facto genitor coniunxque coactae:
"quam" dixit "veniam vos datis, ipsa nego." 830
nec mora, celato fixit sua pectora ferro
et cadit in patrios sanguinulenta pedes.
tunc quoque iam moriens ne non procumbat honeste,
respicit: haec etiam cura cadentis erat.
ecce super corpus communia damna gementes 835
obliti decoris virque paterque iacent.
Brutus adest tandemque animo sua nomina fallit
fixaque semianimi corpore tela rapit
stillantemque tenens generoso sanguine cultrum
edidit impavidos ore minante sonos: 840
"per tibi ego hunc iuro fortem castumque cruorem
perque tuos manes, qui mihi numen erunt,
Tarquinium profuga poenas cum stirpe daturum.
iam satis est virtus dissimulata diu."
illa iacens ad verba oculos sine lumine movit 845
visaque concussa dicta probare coma.
fertur in exsequias animi matrona virilis
et secum lacrimas invidiamque trahit.
volnus inane patet. Brutus clamore Quirites
concitat et regis facta nefanda refert. 850
Tarquinius cum prole fugit; capit annua consul
iura: dies regnis illa suprema fuit.

fallimur, an veris praenuntia venit hirundo
nec metuit, ne qua versa recurrat hiems?
saepe tamen, Procne, nimium properasse quereris, 855
virque tuo Tereus frigore laetus erit.

27. B EQ. NP

Iamque duae restant noctes de mense secundo,
Marsque citos iunctis curribus urget equos:
ex vero positum permansit Equirria nomen,
quae deus in Campo prospicit ipse suo. 860

iure venis, Gradive: locum tua tempora poscunt,
   signatusque tuo nomine mensis adest.
venimus in portum libro cum mense peracto:
   naviget hinc alia iam mihi linter aqua.

Commentary

1-18. Prologue. Ovid's turn from frivolous to serious themes. Dedication to Augustus.

1. **Ianus** = *mensis Iani*, January, named after the god Janus.
  et = *etiam*.
2. **ut:** "just as."
  liber: noun. Note how the line's parallel phrases occur in reverse order (*alter . . . mensis: liber alter* = AB:BA). This common device is called chiasmus, named after the Greek letter χ (chi), which is formed if one places the two phrases one above the other and draws lines to connect the related words.
  eat: < *eo*, "go." Jussive subjunctive.
3. **velis:** < *velum*, "sail"; ablative of means. Ovid frequently compares his poetry to a ship.
  elegi: "elegiac verses"; vocative.
4. **exiguum:** "slight, small," both in length and in theme.
5. **faciles:** here, "compliant."
  in amore ministros: i.e., when Ovid wrote his early love elegies, the *Amores*, and his mock-didactic *Ars amatoria*.
6. **lusit:** < *ludo*, "play."
  numeris . . . suis: Ovid frequently arranges nouns and modifiers in this way at the ends of the pentameter's halves (cf. 12, 16, 30, 34, 36). Similar patterns are often found in hexameters.
  numeris: "meters, verses."
  prima iuventa: sc. *mea*.
7. **idem:** nominative; "the same (poet)." *Idem* is often used where English would use an adverb (e.g., "yet," "also") to emphasize an additional attribute or action.
  sacra: "sacred rites."

8. **ecquis:** an "impassioned interrogative" (*L&S*); = *num quis:* "(Was there) anyone who . . .?".
illinc: "from there"; i.e., amatory elegy.
crederet: deliberative subjunctive, more usual in the first person (*AG* 444).
9. **militia:** "military service, soldiership."
9-10. ferimus, possumus, nostra: first person plurals with singular meaning, as often (cf. 13-16).
9. **quae possumus arma:** relative clauses very frequently come before their antecedents (cf. 23, 65, 119).
10. **dextra:** sc. *manus*
munere: here, "service, duty." Ablative (of separation) with *vacat* ("is free from").
11. **mihi:** dative of agent, not uncommon in poetry with passives besides the gerundive.
12-13. **nec:** Ovid unites three clauses by emphatically repeating the initial word, a figure of speech called anaphora (cf. 63, 85-87).
12. **terga:** poetic plural (i.e., = singular), especially common with parts of the body.
14. **habilis:** "skillful, expert."
quilibet: "anyone."
15. **at:** here, "yet, still" (*L&S* II.D [a]).
prosequimur: "I pursue (the theme of)."
studioso: "eager, zealous."
pectore: < *pectus,* "breast" (as the seat of emotions and/or intellect); "heart, mind."
Caesar: Augustus Caesar.
16. **nomina:** "titles" or "honors."
per . . . tuos: "and I proceed all along (the road dotted with) tablets (commemorating your glorious achievements)." *Titulus* = "tablet, inscription, title." Enclitic -*que* unites the clauses but is postponed (as frequently by Ovid).
17. **ades:** singular imperative < *adsum,* "stand by, assist (me)"; often addressed to a deity.
placido: here, "kindly."
18. **pacando:** "subduing"; gerundive modifying *hoste* (construction equivalent to gerund + direct object).
si quid . . . vacas: "if you are free at all"; i.e., "if you have any time to spare." *quid* is adverbial.
hoste: collective.

19-46. Derivation of the word "February."

19. **dixere** = *dixerunt*, a common variant form; here, "called."
   piamina: < *piamen*, "means/instrument of purification"; direct object (the synonym *februa* is predicate accusative).
   patres: here, "forefathers."
20. **verbo:** "(the meaning of) the word" (Frazer).
   fidem: "proof."
21. **rege:** i.e., the *rex sacrorum*, a priest.
   flamine: a priest in charge of the rites of a specific deity; here probably the *flamen Dialis*, "the priest of Jupiter," although the rite is not elsewhere known.
   lanas: "objects made of wool."
22. **quis** = **quibus**; dative of possession, frequent with *nomen est* (cf. 25).
   veterum lingua: "in the language of the ancients."
23. **quaeque ... purgamina** = *et purgamina quae*.
   lictor: the "attendant" of certain officials, here perhaps of the *flamen Dialis*.
   purgamina = *piamina* (see on 19).
   versis: < *verro*, "sweep out"; in ablative absolute with *domibus*. The text is disputed.
24. **torrida:** "parched, toasted."
   mica: "grain, bit"; sc. *salis*.
   farra: < *far*, "spelt," a kind of wheat; in apposition with *purgamina* (23).
25. **nomen idem:** sc. *est*. The ellipsis or omission of *sum* in all its parts is very common (cf. 31, 56, etc.).
26. **tempora:** "temples (of the head)."
27. **flaminicam:** "the wife of a *flamen*."
28. **poscentl:** sc. *flaminicae*.
29. **denique:** "in short"; frequently used with this meaning in generalizing conclusions (*L&S* II.B.2).
   piantur: here, "are purified" (cf. *piamina* 19).
31. **his:** sc. *februis*.
   dictus: sc. *est;* "(was) named."
   secta ... pelle: i.e., a strip of hide, strap.
   Luperci: youths celebrating the feast of the Lupercalia on February 15 who struck the ground and those they met with strips of goat-skins (cf. below 267ff. and *OCD* s.v. "Lupercalia.").
32. **solum:** "the ground."
   id: the antecedent is the activity just referred to.
   habent: "they regard/treat (as)."

33.   placatis: < *placo,* "appease, propitiate."
34.   ferales . . . dies: "the days devoted to the dead" (Frazer), i.e., the Feralia on February 21, which marks the end of the *dies parentales* in honor of the dead which began on the 13th (see 533 ff.).
   praeteriere: < *praetereo,* "go by, pass." For the ending see on 19.
35.   purgamina: subject of *posse* in indirect statement.
36.   tollere: "remove."
   senes: here, "ancestors."
37.   moris: < *mos,* "custom."
   illa = *Graecia.*
   nocentis: "guilty people" (< *noceo,* "harm"); accusative subject of *ponere* in indirect statement.
38.   impia: modifies *facta* ("deeds").
   ponere = *deponere,* as often.
39.   Actoriden: sc. *solvit* (here, "cleansed") from 40; such ellipsis in parallel clauses occurs frequently. The suffix *-ides* (*-iden,* Greek accusative ending) is a patronymic indicating a person's lineage; here Patroclus, grandson of Actor, is meant. After accidentally killing the (variously named) son of Amphidamas of Opus, the youth Patroclus fled to Phthia, where he was granted refuge by King Peleus and began his famous relationship with Achilles.
   Peleus: disyllabic and spondaic, as is *Aegeus* in 41. Understand *et* before *ipsum.* Such asyndeton (omission of a coordinating conjunction) is very common.
   Pelea: Greek accusative; trisyllabic and dactylic.
40.   per: "by means of."
   Haemonias: "Thessalian." After his unintentional murder of Phocus at the Calydonian boar hunt, Peleus took refuge with Acastus, king of Iolcus in Thessaly.
41.   vectam: < *veho;* agrees with *Phasida* (42).
   inane: "empty space," i.e., "the air."
42.   immerita . . . ope: "undeserved aid."
   Phasida: accusative (cf. *Pelea* 39). Medea is called "Phasian" after the river Phasis in her native land Colchis. She fled to (and was married by) King Aegeus of Athens after murdering her children in Corinth.
   fovit: here, "supported, befriended."
43.   An unusual hexameter, composed of only three words (all Greek names), ending with a word of more than three syllables, and with the avoidance of elision (hiatus) in the fifth foot. It is to be scanned:

$$\text{Amphiareiādēs Naupactōō Achelōō}$$

Amphiareiades: Alcmaeon, son of Amphiaraus, was pursued by the Erinyes for the murder of his mother until he was purified by the river-god Achelous.

Naupactoo: "Naupactian." Naupactus was located in western Locris on the Corinthian Gulf.

44.   ille = *Achelous*. *Ille* denotes a change of subject, as often.
45.   faciles: here, "ready (to believe), credulous."

47-54. February's position in the calendar. Ovid asserts that though January was always the first month, February was originally the twelfth; and that the decemvirs (see on 54) moved February to follow January as the second month. Scholars now tend to reject this statement, although the decemvirs probably did institute a major change in the calendar. Ovid elsewhere (1.43-44) contradicts himself by claiming that King Numa added January and February to the beginning of an older ten-month year.

48.   et: See on 1.
49.   qui: sc. *is* or *mensis*. The antecedent of a relative pronoun is often omitted when it can be easily supplied from the context (cf. 52).
   sequitur: Note present tense.
50.   quoque: goes closely with *sacrorum*. I.e., Terminus, the god of boundaries, also marked the "boundary" or "end" of the year's religious festivals. If this is meant to be taken literally, Ovid has in mind the pre-Julian practice of inserting an intercalary "month" in some years after February 23 (the date of the Terminalia; cf. 639ff.) in order to keep the calendar in line with planetary movements. The remainder of February was counted as part of the intercalary period.
   Termine: The narrator addresses Terminus directly, a very common Ovidian device (apostrophe).
52.   imis: "lowest, below" but *imus*, "last"; a pun.
   manibus: < *manes*, "the shades, spirits of the underworld." See on 34.
53.   spatio . . . longo: i.e., the period from March through December.
54.   tempora: January and February.
   bis quini . . . viri: the *decemviri legibus scribundis* ("the commission of 10 men appointed for the purpose of writing the laws") who prepared the Twelve Tables in the middle of the fifth century B.C.

continuasse = *continuavisse*, "to have connected." Such syncopation or shortening in the perfect system is common.

55-72. February 1. (For an explanation of the symbols identifying each day as it occurs in the calendar, see the introduction.)

55. Phrygiae . . . Matri: (the Temple of) the Magna Mater, Cybele, whose cult was brought to Rome from Phrygia in the late third century. Dative after *contermina*. The use of a deity's name for his or her temple is not uncommon.

56. Sospita = *Iuno Sospita*, "Juno the Savior"; again, the name represents the temple.

delubris: < *delubrum*, "shrine"; poetic plural, as is *templa* in 58.

aucta [sc. **esse**]: "to have been honored" (< *augeo*, "increase").

57. sint: subjunctive in indirect question introduced by *quaeris*.

Kalendis: "the Kalends," the first day of a month, always sacred to Juno. Ablative of time.

58. procubuere: < *procumbo*, "fall down."
die: here, "time."

59. The *ne*-clause is governed by *cavit* (60): "took care that . . . not."

60. sacrati . . . ducis: Augustus, who had directed an extensive program of restoring religious buildings. In his *Res Gestae* 20.4 he claimed to have repaired 82 temples in the year 28 B.C.

61. delubris: dative (see on 11).

62. nec satis est: sc. *obligare* from the second half of the line; here, "to place under an obligation/do favors for."

64. sit: jussive subjunctive in a clause in apposition with *opto*.
superis: "for the gods above"; dative of possession.
tui: objective genitive with *cura*.

65. caelestes: "the heavenly gods"; subject of *dent*.
quos: sc. *dedisti*.

66. tua: modifies *domo*.
in statione: "on guard." Ovid may have in mind the deities Apollo and Vesta. The former's great temple on the Palatine Hill was adjacent to Augustus' residence--and also contained representations of Diana and Latona; a shrine to the latter was located near (or perhaps in) the house.

67. celebratur: "is crowded/thronged."

Helerni: The entire couplet is obscure. It is not known whether Helernus is the name of a deity or (as explanatory genitive) the grove, or to what exactly it is supposed to be "near" (*vicini*); the Tiber? Ostia? The pentameter seems to refer to the mouth of the Tiber at Ostia (about 16 miles from Rome), but Ovid in the *Fasti* rarely mentions Italian rites so distant from Rome.

68. qua: "where."
 petit: "heads toward."
 advena Thybris: "the foreign Tiber," usually explained as referring to the river's path from Etruria to Rome. But since the grove is near the sea, *advena* may refer more literally to the Tiber "arriving at" (cf. *advenio*) the Tyrrhenian.

69. ad penetrale Numae: "at the sanctuary of Numa" = the Temple of Vesta in the Roman Forum, whose shrine was thought to have been located originally in the palace of Rome's second king (cf. *Tristia* 3.1.29-30). Ovid may also mean "near" the Regia, the headquarters of the *pontifex maximus* in the vicinity of Vesta's Temple and traditionally believed to have been Numa's palace.
 Capitolinumque Tonantem: sc. *Iovem;* "and (the Temple of) Jupiter the Thunderer on the Capitoline Hill." See on 55.

70. summa ... arce: "on the top of the citadel"; i.e., at the top of the Capitoline, where the Temple of Jupiter Optimus Maximus was located.
 bidens: "sacrificial animal."

71. adopertus: < *adoperio,* "cover, hide."
 auster: "south wind."

72. posita: "fallen" (Frazer).
 nive: < *nix,* "snow."

73-78. February 2. The Constellations Lyra ("the Lyre") and Leo ("the Lion").

73. proximus: with adverbial force, as commonly with adjectives modifying subject or object.
 Hesperias: "western."
 Titan: "the sun(-god)."
 abiturus: < *abeo.*
 in undas: The sun and stars were imagined to rise from and fall (or set) into the ocean (cf. 78, 149 & 192).

74. cum: "when," governing the whole couplet.
 equis: The sun and stars are regularly described as travelling by horse or chariot (cf. 314 & 458).

76. The constellation Lyra has set, i.e., disappeared below the horizon.

    Lyra: subject of *est*. It has been "attracted" into the relative clause.

    fulsit: < *fulgeo*, "shine."

77. medii ... terga Leonis: *medii* is a transferred epithet that belongs logically, but not syntactically, to *terga* (plural for singular). It is unclear whether Ovid means that only half of the constellation or the entire constellation has disappeared from view.

78. mersa [sc. **esse**]: < *mergo*, "plunge, sink." The passive here has a reflexive force like the Greek middle voice: "has plunged itself," i.e., "has sunk/set."

79-118. February 3. Arion and the Dolphin.

79. modo: adverb, "just now."

    caelatum: < *caelo*, "engrave, adorn."

    Delphina: Greek accusative (as are *Lesbida* [82] and *Ariona* [83]), antecedent of *quem*, but attracted into the relative clause and to the case of the relative pronoun; repeated by *is* in 80: *Quem ... Delphina ... is = Delphin quem*.

80. visus: accusative plural.

81-82. The couplet goes logically with *caelatum stellis* in 79 rather than with line 80.

81. felix ... index: "fortunate informer." The Dolphin found and revealed the hiding, frightened sea-nymph Amphitrite to her would-be lover Neptune; he is called *felix* because of his consequent rise to the sky as a constellation.

82. Lesbida: "Lesbian." Arion hailed from Methymna on the island Lesbos.

    domino: < *dominus*, "owner."

83. novit: < *nosco*, "get to know"; the perfect regularly has the force of a present, hence here, "knows."

85. a voce = *ab eo canente*.

86. restitit: < *resisto*, "stop, come to a standstill."

87. lepores: < *lepus*, "hare."

89. lite: < *lis*, "quarrel, wrangling."

    Palladis alite: "the bird of Pallas (= the Roman Minerva)," the owl, natural enemy and (because of its silence) proverbial opposite of the crow. Ovid elsewhere notes that the crow had once been Minerva's favorite bird, before it gave the goddess offence and was replaced by the owl.

90. accipitri: "hawk"; dative.
91. Cynthia = *Diana*, so called from the mountain Cynthus on the island Delos, where she was born with her brother Apollo, the god of music.
   tuis: sc. *modis* from 92 (here, "melodies, music"); ablative with *obstipuisse* ("to have been astonished").
   fertur: "is said," a common meaning of *fero*.
93-94. impleverat . . . captaque erat: Ovid regularly begins the narrative proper with pluperfects (or imperfects) that sketch background information or set the scene.
93. nomen Arionium: "the name of Arion." Latin is fond of adjectival forms of proper nouns where we would use a genitive.
   Siculas: "Sicilian."
94. capta: "charmed" (Frazer).
   Ausonis: "Ausonian" = "Italian"; modifies *ora*.
95. inde: "from there."
   puppem: "stern"; but = *navem* by synecdoche (the use of part of something to stand for the whole, or *vice versa*).
96. quaesitas: "won, gained" (< *quaero*).
   opes: "wealth."
97. infelix: vocative.
99. destricto: < *destringo*, here "draw."
100. conscia: "conspiring."
101. quid tibi cum gladio: sc. *est*. Idiom: *esse* + dative + *cum* (+ ablative of a person or thing) = "for someone to have a relationship/business with someone/thing." "What business do you have with a sword?" "What are you doing with a sword?" (cf. 308).
   dubiam: "wavering, tottering."
   rege: < *rego;* imperative.
102. tenenda: gerundive expressing necessity.
103. ille = *Arion*. See on 44.
104. sumpta . . . lyra: ablative absolute logically dependent on *liceat*: "let me take up my lyre and sing a little."
105. dant veniam: "they give (him) permission." The tense changes to historical present (= perfect), a vivid (and common) means of narrating past events. This commentary glosses verbs in the historical present as present tense.
106. possit: subjunctive in relative clause of characteristic.
   Phoebe: vocative; apostrophe to Phoebus Apollo.
   decere: "to suit, grace, adorn."
107. induerat: < *induo*, "put on."

Tyrio bis tinctam murice: "twice dyed with Tyrian purple," i.e., even more expensive than an ordinary purple garment. The *murex* was a fish from which purple dye was extracted. The color was often called "Tyrian" after the famous dye-works at the Phoenecian city of Tyre. *tinctam* < *tingo*.

108. pollice: < *pollex*, "thumb."
  chorda: singular for plural, "strings."
109. canentia: "white," modifying *tempora*.
109-110. dura ... penna: ablative. *penna*: usually "feather" or "wing," but here "arrow."
110. tempora: accusative of specification or respect, sometimes called the Greek accusative, frequently used to express the bodily part affected; with *traiectus* (< *traicio*, "transfix"). Lit., "transfixed as to the temples"; translate "pierced in the temple(s)."
  olor: "swan."
111. ornatus: "dressed in all his finery."
  desilit: another switch to historical present (see on 105), here at the climax of the narrative.
112. impulsa: < *impello*; "struck" evidently by the leaping Arion. The participle may also be transferred (see on 77) from *puppis*, as *caerula* seems to be from *aqua*.
113. inde: "then, next."
  fide maius: "(this is) beyond belief."
  delphina: subject of *supposuisse* in indirect statement.
114. memorant: "they (i.e., people in general) say."
  oneri: dative with the compound *supposuisse*.
115. citharamque: The *-que* introduces the first of 3 coordinate clauses and has little connective force.
115-116. pretium vehendi cantat: lit., "he sings the price of transporting"; = *carmine pretium vehendi solvit*. *Vehendi* is objective genitive.
117. astris: "into the constellations." *Recipere* + ablative = "to admit (someone) to friendship, citizenship, or other status" (*OLD* s.v. *recipio* 2).

119-144. February 5. Augustus as *pater patriae*.

119. mihi: dative with the compound *inesse*.
  sonos: "voices."
  quoque = *quo* + *-que*. The antecedent is *pectus* (120), with which the *-que* logically belongs.

120. vellem: "I could wish"; potential subjunctive, in which the imperfect usually refers to past time, but *vellem* and *mallem* express an unfulfilled wish in the present.

Maeonide: "the Lydian," i.e., the poet Homer, who was often said to have come from Lydia, sometimes called Maeonia. Vocative.

pectus: here roughly "lungs" (as the characteristic organ of a poet's power); cf. 15.

121. alterno pectine: "with the music alternating (between hexameters and pentameters)"; i.e., in the elegiac meter. *Pecten* is literally an instrument for striking the lyre.

Nonas: < *Nonae*, "the Nones," the name of the fifth day of a month (except March, May, July, October, when they were the seventh), so called because they always fall nine days (counting inclusively) before the day of the month known as the Ides.

122. accumulatur: "is heaped on" or "is added (to)."

honos: refers either to the Augustan title mentioned below, or to Ovid's treatment of the subject.

123. ingenium: sc. *meum*.

maioraque viribus urgent [sc. me]: "and things greater than (my) strength burden (me)"; i.e., "and the burden is greater than my strength can bear."

124. mihi: dative of agent in passive periphrastic.

praecipuo . . . ore: i.e., "with a special poetic effort."

125. quid: "why?"

demens: "out of my mind."

elegis: dative governed by compound verb.

125-126. tantum ponderis: "such a great burden"; *ponderis* is genitive of the whole (also known as partitive genitive).

126. heroi . . . pedis: "(the task) of heroic verse"; genitive of description as predicate. Heroic verse is dactylic hexameter, the meter of epic poetry.

heroi: scanned as three long syllables.

127. pater patriae: an honorific title bestowed upon Augustus on February 5, 2 B.C.

curia: "the senate house"; i.e., "the senate." (An example of metonomy, the use of the name of something to indicate something associated with it.)

128. eques: collective, in apposition with *nos;* "the equestrian order, the knights." Ovid switches to the first person since he himself was an *eques*.

129. res: "the fact, reality"; i.e., "your deeds."

sero: adverb; "late."

tulisti: < *fero*, here "receive."
130. iam pridem ... eras: With expressions of duration of time the imperfect denotes an action continuing in the past but begun previously; "you had been already for a long time."
orbis = *orbis terrarum*, "of the world."
131. hoc: with *nomen* in 132.
per terras: "throughout the earth." This plural commonly denotes earth in the sense "world."
Iuppiter: sc. *habet*.
132. deum: genitive plural.
133-144. Romule: an elaborate comparison of Romulus and Augustus addressed to Romulus himself (the founder and first king of Rome).
133. concedes: The future is almost a command; "you must yield/give way (to Augustus)."
hic = Augustus.
magna: predicate accusative.
tuendo: < *tueor*, "guard"; ablative of the gerund.
134. tu ... Remo: The precise syntax is uncertain, but the sense is definitely contemptuous. Either gerundive and understood object (*moenia*) express purpose, as commonly after *do*, and *Remo* is indirect object; or the gerundive denotes propriety ("[only] fit to be leapt across") and *Remo* is dative of agent. Remus defiantly leapt over the new city walls, for which action (in most accounts) his twin brother Romulus killed him.
135. te ... sensit: "felt you(r power)." Two or more subjects may take a singular verb when the verb belongs properly with one subject (often the nearest) and is understood with the other(s).
Tatius: king of the Sabines, an ancient Italian people.
Cures: nominative plural; capital town of the early Sabines.
Caenina: a small town east of Rome.
136. hoc duce: ablative absolute.
solis ... latus: "either side of the sun"; i.e., whichever side of the earth the sun is shining on.
137. nescio quid: "something," i.e., "a little bit"; sometimes written as one word.
138. Iove = *caelo* by metonomy (see on 127).
139. rapis: sc. *maritas* ("brides"). A reference to the legendary Rape of the Sabines by Romulus and his men. The Romans seized young Sabine women visiting at a Roman festival to be their brides. Cf. below 431ff.

castas: predicate adjective. Ovid refers to the legislation promulgated by Augustus against adultery.

140. luco: ablative (see on 117); the Asylum, an enclosed area between the two summits of the Capitoline Hill that Romulus supposedly made available to refugees from neighboring communities in an effort to increase Rome's population.

nefas: "crime"; i.e., criminals.

141. vis: "force, violence"; commonly used of civil violence.

142. domini: "master"; especially derogatory, since the people under such a ruler would be "slaves."

principis: < *princeps*, "leading citizen, first among equals"; the preferred title of Augustus.

143. te Remus incusat: i.e., of murdering him (see on 134).

144. caelestem: "a god"; predicate accusative after *fecit*.

pater: Mars, through whose intercession with Jupiter his son Romulus was deified. The story is told below 481-512.

patrem: Julius Caesar, the adoptive father of Augustus, was declared to be a god by the senate after his death.

145-148. The constellation Aquarius and a weather-sign.

145. puer Idaeus: Ganymede, called "Idaean" after Mount Ida near Troy, where he was carried off by Jupiter to be the cupbearer of the gods. The mythological character is here identified with the astronomical figure Aquarius or the Water-Carrier, who appears in the sky pouring liquid from a jug.

tenus: "down to"; preposition governing *media . . . alvo*, "the middle of (his) belly."

eminet: here, "becomes/is visible."

147. en: interjection; with imperatives = "come on now."

siquis: "if anyone"; sometimes written as two words. The indefinite pronoun *quis, quid* (instead of *aliquis, -quid*) is normally used after *si, ne, num* and *nisi*.

Borean: Greek accusative of *Boreas*, "the north wind" (of winter).

148. Zephyris: < *Zephyrus*, "the west wind."

149-152. February 9. The advent of spring.

149-150. Quintus . . . Lucifer: the fifth day after the Nones on February 5. This is the ninth, since the Romans included the point of departure as well as the end-point in their counting. *Lucifer:* "the morning star, day"; "five days later the morning star has lifted up its radiance . . . " (Frazer).

  extulit . . . et . . . erunt = *cum . . . extulit, erunt.* An example of parataxis (the juxtaposition of gramatically independent clauses or sentences) in which one clause is logically dependent upon the other.

150. primi: "the beginning of."
  veris: < *ver, veris* (neuter), "spring."
151. ne: the purpose clause depends logically on an idea like "know that" or "let me tell you that" which implicitly introduces *restant tibi . . .* (cf. 47).

  fallare = *fallaris* (< *fallo,* "deceive"); *-re* is a common variant of the 2nd singular passive present system ending.

  restant: < *resto,* "remain, lie in store"; the second *restant* has the sense "indeed they do."

  frigora: "frosts."
152. signa: here, "traces."

153-192. February 11. The constellations Arctophylax (Boötes) and Ursa Maior.

153. veniat: jussive subjunctive.
  Custodem . . . Ursae: "the Guardian of the Bear," the northern constellation more commonly known by its Greek names Arctophylax and (when regarded as a herdsman) Boötes.
154. geminos exseruisse pedes: "has thrust forth both his feet" (Frazer). The imagined figure of the *Custos* rises (i.e., first appears over the horizon) lying down.
155. hamadryadas: "forest-nymphs."
  iaculatricem: < *iaculatrix,* "spear-thrower, huntress."
156. pars: "member, participant."
  chori: A band of nymphs is often referred to as a *chorus* (lit., a group performing a song and dance).
157. arcus: accusative (and poetic) plural. Callisto touches a sacred symbol of the goddess, as others lay their hands on a deity's altar when making an oath. The second *arcus* is vocative.
158. este: plural imperative of *sum.*
159. Cynthia: See on 91.
159-60. serva, et . . . eris: The paratactic imperative and future clauses are roughly equivalent to a future more vivid condition.
160. princeps: "foremost."
  mihi: dative of reference or possession.

161. servasset = servavisset (see on 54) in a past contrary-to-fact condition.

162. cavit: < *caveo*, here "keep clear of."

de: sc. an adversative conjunction, e.g., *autem*, omitted by asyndeton (see on 39).

de Iove crimen habet: lit., "she has blame concerning Jupiter"; i.e., "Jupiter had raped her, and she was blamed for unchastity as a result."

163. feras: < *fera*, "wild beast."

Phoebe = *Diana*.

venata: < *venor*, "hunt."

164. aut plus [sc. **diei**] **aut medium . . . diem:** either after noon or at noon. The ablative absolute governs the whole line.

165. ut: "when," + indicative.

tetigit: < *tango*, "touch, reach."

densa . . . ilice: ablative of specification with *niger*.

lucus: sc. *erat*.

167. hic: "here."

Tegeaea: "of Tegea," a town in Arcadia.

lavemur: "let us wash ourselves"; passive with reflexive force (see on 78).

168. virginis: explanatory genitive with *sono* (here, "name").

169. velamina: < *velamen*, "covering, clothing."

ponunt: See on 38.

170. hanc pudet: "it shames (her)"; i.e., "she is ashamed."

171-72. uteri . . . suo: lit., "conspicuous with the swelling of her belly, she is given away by her own disclosure of the weight (she bears)." *Suo* may be transferred from *ponderis* (see on 77). *Manifesta* also has associations of "guilty."

173. cui: A relative pronoun is frequently used at the beginning of a sentence to connect it with the preceding sentence.

periura: < *periurus*, "oath-breaking."

Lycaoni: < *Lycaonis*, "daughter of Lycaon" (legendary king of Arcadia); vocative.

174. nec . . . pollue: Negatives with the imperative are common in poetry.

175. implerat = **impleverat** (see on 54). Ten lunar months (the length of a pregnancy as measured by the Romans) had passed.

cornibus: The tips (and stages) of the crescent moon were regularly called "horns."

176. quae ... credita = *ea quae credita erat virgo esse. fuerat*.
.. credita = *credita erat; fui* is a common variant for *sum* as auxiliary verb in the perfect, and *fueram* for *eram* in the pluperfect (cf. 182).
177. laesa: "injured," because her husband has fathered a child by someone else.
178. facis: apostrophe to Juno.
   est ... passa: < *patior*, "suffer"; here, "submitted to sexual intercourse with" (cf. *OLD* 2c).
179. utque: "and when"; see on 165.
   paelice: < *paelex*, "mistress, rival."
180. eat: See on 2.
181. squalida: "shaggy, rough."
182. summo ... Iovi: dative of agent (see on 11).
183. lustra: < *lustrum*, "a five-year period," so called after the religious ceremony of purification or lustration (cf. *lustrant*, 32) performed every five years following the census.
   furto: either the adverb "secretly" or ablative of *furtum* in the sense "secret love affair."
   agebat: With a specified number of years **agere** = "to be in (a given year), to be (so) old."
184. est obvia facta: < *obvius fio*, "meet" (+ dative).
185. tamquam: "as if," followed by subjunctive in a conditional clause of comparison. *Illa* remains the subject.
   amens: "frantic."
187. fixisset: < *figo*, "pierce."
188. ni foret = *nisi esset;* i.e., if both had not been made into constellations.
189. signa: here, "constellations"; in apposition with the unexpressed subject of *micant:* "they gleam as neighboring constellations."
   prior est: "she is ahead (of him)" as they appear in the sky.
   Arcton: "the bear"; Greek accusative.
190. Arctophylax: See on 153; nominative.
   terga: sc. *ursae*.
   sequentis: "of (one) following."
191. adhuc: "still" (adverb).
   canam: "white(-haired), old"; with *Tethyn* (Greek accusative of *Tethys*, sea-goddess and wife of Ocean).
   Saturnia: "Saturnian," a common epithet of Juno, Saturn's daughter. Subject of both *saevit* and *rogat*.
192. Maenaliam: "Maenalian, of Maenalus," a mountain in Arcadia; modifies *Arcton*.

tactis: modifies *aquis*, but logically coordinate with *lavet:* "not to touch and wash the Maenalian Bear with (her) waters." Ovid explains why Ursa Major (the back and tail of which are our Big Dipper) never sets. It is one of the north circumpolar constellations, i.e., those always in view in the northern temperate zone, appearing to wheel around the North Star.

193-242. February 13. Sacrifice to Faunus. The Fabii.

193. Idibus: "the Ides," name of the thirteenth day of the month except in March, May, July and October, when they fell on the fifteenth; ablative of time when.

agrestis: "rustic"; modifies *Fauni* (< *Faunus*, a minor Italian deity of herdsmen and forests).

altaria: < *altaria, -ium*, "top part of an altar, altar."

194. discretas: < *discerno*, "separate, part."

insula: sc. *Tiberina*, the island in the river Tiber opposite the Capitoline Hill.

195ff. Early in the fifth century when Rome was on the verge of waging several wars at once, the Fabii family voluntarily took over the war against Veii, an Etruscan city nine miles north of Rome. It is worth comparing Ovid's account with that of the historian Livy (2.48-50), whom he follows.

195. illa: "that famous."

Veientibus: < *Veiens*, here an adjective, "of Veii."

196. ter centum ... ter ... duo: i.e., 306; sc. *et* before the second *ter*.

cecidere: < *cado*, "fall"; for the ending see on 19.

197. vires et onus susceperat: an example of zeugma ("joining"), the use of a word to govern or modify two words in different senses: the family "had undertaken (to provide) the military forces (*vires*)" and "had undertaken (to shoulder) the burden."

198. gentiles: < *gentilis*, "of a clan/family (*gens*)."

professa: < *profiteor;* either in a passive sense, "promised" (*OLD* 3a), or perhaps "that promise (a combat)" (*L&S* II.D).

199. castris: lit., "camp"; i.e., house or meeting place in the city.

miles: collective.

generosus: not "generous" but "noble, of good family/stock."

200. e quis = *e quibus*. The antecedent is the plural idea in *miles* (199); goes with *quilibet:* "any one of whom."

dux fieri: with *aptus,* "capable, fit." In poetry many adjectives take an infinitive.

201. "the nearest way [out of Rome to Veii] is by the right-hand arch of Carmentis' gate." The Porta Carmentalis was named after the goddess Carmentis whose shrine was nearby.

dextro . . . iano: ablative of way by which or route.

202. ire . . . noli: "do not go"; regular form of the negative imperative in prose (contrast 174).

omen habet: "it has a (bad) omen, it is ominous."

203. illa: sc. *via;* ablative of route (cf. 201).

refert: "reports, says."

exisse = *exiisse* (< *exeo*), a frequent shortening.

204. culpa: ablative with *vacat* (see on 10).

205. Cremeram: < *Cremera,* a stream near Veii.

rapacem: lit., "ravenous"; as an epithet of rivers, "wild."

207. loco: sc. *illo.*

ponunt: "pitch."

207-208. destrictis . . . eunt: Ovid's rapid narrative is elliptical. The Fabii are repelling an attack on their camp.

208. Tyrrhenum . . . agmen: "Etruscan battle-line."

valido Marte: lit., "with a mighty warlike spirit" (*OLD* s.v. Mars 5), i.e., bravely fighting.

per . . . eunt = *perrumpunt.*

209. non aliter quam cum: "not otherwise than when"; a typical introductory formula for a simile.

Libyca: "Libyan."

210. greges: < *grex,* "flock."

211. tergo: Singular for plural of a bodily part is very common when referring to a group (cf. 234).

212. Tusco: < *Tuscus,* "Tuscan, Etruscan."

213. aperte: "openly," i.e., meeting face to face in the open field.

214. non datur: impersonal; sc. *Etruscis* (dative).

insidias armaque tecta: an example of the figure called hendiadys (= "one through two," i.e., the use of two nouns with a conjunction instead of one modified noun); = *insidias armorum tectorum. tecta* < *tego,* here "hide."

215. ultima: neuter plural accusative; "limits, boundary, rim."

216. occulere: "to conceal"; with *apta* (see on 200).

217. paucos: sc. *milites.*

rara: "scattered, here and there."

218. cetera . . . turba: i.e., the rest of their forces.

219. ecce: interjection vividly introducing a new event; "lo, behold."
  torrens: "a torrent, wild stream."
  auctus: "increased"; i.e., "swollen."
220. Zephyro: See on 148.
  victa: "conquered"; i.e., "melted."
221. sata: "crops, fields."
  fertur: passive with reflexive force; "carries itself (swiftly)"; i.e., "runs, flows swiftly."
222. riparum: with *margine* ("border").
  clausas: modifies the object *aquas*, but refers to the same activity as the verb *finit*. Translate: "does not confine and enclose the waters . . ."
223. latis discursibus: lit., "with wide runnings about"; i.e., "running in different directions."
224. sternunt: "they lay low, kill."
  metus alter: either = *metus aliorum* (Bömer; Peter) or "fear of a second enemy (i.e., in ambush)" (Hallam).
  inest: sc. *Fabiis*.
225. quo: "where, to what place?"
  ruitis: "are you rushing"; apostrophe to the Fabii at the critical point of the narrative.
  male: i.e., your trust will result in your misfortune.
226. simplex: "unsuspecting."
227. virtus: "valor, bravery."
228. latus: < *latus, lateris*.
229. quid faciant: "what are they to do?"; deliberative subjunctive.
230. quidve: "or what"; *-ve* ("or") is a conjunctive enclitic like *que*.
  restet: subjunctive in relative clause of characteristic.
231. longe: "far and wide."
  Laurentibus: "of Laurentum," a town in Latium (see on 270) southwest of Rome. The woodlands around Laurentum were a prime hunting ground for the delicacy of wild boar.
232. fulmineo . . . ore: "(its) lightning-quick tusks" (*OLD*), "flashing teeth" (Bömer), "thunderous snout" (Frazer), "flashing tusk" (Hallam).
233. inulti: "unavenged"; sc. *Fabii*.
234. -que . . . -que . . . -que: "and . . . both . . . and."
  alterna . . . manu: "alternately"; *manu* applies logically only to *dant*.
  ferunt: See on 129.

236. perdidit: < *perdo,* "lose, destroy."
237. ut ... superessent: noun clause, object of *consuluisse* ("took care [that]") in 238. Secondary sequence is usual after the perfect infinitive depending on a primary tense.
   Herculeae: "of Hercules," from whom the Fabii claimed descent, just as other prominent Roman families claimed to be descended from other gods or mythological heroes.
   semina: < *semen,* "seed."
238. deos: accusative subject of *consuluisse.*
239. impubes: "pre-adolescent"; masculine singular nominative.
   utilis: here, "fit."
240. unus: "alone, the only one."
241. scilicet: "clearly, undoubtedly."
   olim: here, "one day, some day."
   Maxime: Ovid apostrophizes the most famous member of the Fabian gens, Quintus Fabius Maximus Cunctator.
242. cui ... foret [= esset]: relative clause of purpose (*cui:* dative of agent).
   res = *res publica.*
   cunctando: < *cunctor,* "delay"; ablative gerund. Quintus Fabius was remembered primarily for his leading role in the Second Punic War: he kept Hannibal at bay by avoiding pitched battles ("delaying"), a strategy that earned him the cognomen Cunctator.

243-266. February 14. The constellations Snake (*Hydra* or *Anguis*), Raven (*Corvus*) and the Bowl (*Crater*). *Hydra* is pictured in the sky as a long constellation with *Crater* on its back and *Corvus* on its tail.

243. Continuata: "joined together, contiguous (with one another)"; sc. *sunt.*
   loco: ablative of specification.
244. et ... iacet: The structure changes in mid-sentence as appositives (*Corvus et Anguis,* 243) give way to an independent clause.
245. Idibus: See on 193.
246. quae ... cur tria = *cur illa tria* (see on 173).
   cur ... sint: indirect question, introduced by *canam.*
247. forte: "by chance."
248. faciet ... moras: "will cause delay"; a joke, since Ovid is telling a story about delay (cf. 249, 256, 259).
249. mea ... avis: the raven, sacred to Apollo, the god of prophecy, because of its reputed prophetic powers.

quid: "anything" (see on 147).
250. tenuem: here, "clear, pure."
vivis: "living" in the sense "running"; a common epithet of water.
251. pedibus: here, "claws."
cratera: < *crater;* Greek accusative singular.
252. aerium pervolat . . . iter: "flies along (his) aerial path"; *iter* is cognate accusative (an object related in meaning to its verb).
aerium: quadrisyllabic.
altus: adjective with adverbial force; "on high, aloft."
253. adhuc: modifies *duris.*
ficus: feminine (as are the names of all trees), "fig tree."
pomis: < *pomum,* "fruit"; ablative of specification with *densissima.*
254. legi: "to be picked"; with *apta.*
255. imperii: < *imperium,* here "command" (of Apollo); genitive governed by *inmemor.*
fertur: See on 91.
256. dum fierent: "(waiting) until they became"; *dum*-clauses implying expectation or intention take the subjunctive. For tense sequence see on 237.
257. satur: "stuffed," i.e., with figs. Nominative.
hydrum: < *hydrus,* "water-snake."
258. ad dominumque = *et ad dominum.*
ficta: "lying, deceptive," < *fingo,* "fashion, invent".
259. hic: sc. *erat.*
obsessor: The word has two meanings, both appropriate here: "one who sits (in/at a place)" and "blockader."
260. tenuit: zeugma (see on 197). The snake "occupied" (or "held control over") the spring and "prevented" the duty from being fulfilled.
261. culpae: sc. *tuae;* dative.
262. fatidicum: "prophetic"; modifies *deum.*
263. tibi: dative of agent.
dum: "while, as long as" (contrast 256).
lactens: "milky"; i.e., unripe.
ficus: here the fruit rather than the tree.
265. monumenta: in apposition with the pentameter; "as (lasting) memorials . . ."

267-452. February 15. Lupercalia.

267. Idus: accusative; see on 193.

nudos . . . Lupercos: The youths celebrating the Lupercalia (see on 31) ran about the Palatine Hill in Rome clad only in girdles of animal skins. Mention of their "nakedness" at the outset announces the major theme of the section (cf. 283ff.).

268. aspicit, et . . . eunt = *cum aspicit, eunt* (see on 149-50).

Fauni: Faunus was the deity celebrated at the Lupercalia (see on 193). He is "two-horned" and has goats' legs like the Greek god Pan, with whom he is here identified.

eunt: here, "come" or "proceed."

269. Pierides: "the daughters of Pierus," the Muses.

quae sit origo: indirect question after *dicite*.

270. attigerint: < *attingo*, "reach, arrive at"; perfect subjunctive.

Latias: < *Latius*, "of/in Latium," the Italian region where Rome is located.

petita: sc. *sacra* from 269; here "fetched" (*OLD* s.v. *peto* 6).

271. Pana: < *Pan* (see on 268); Greek accusative.

pecoris: < *pecus*, "flock, herd."

coluisse: < *colo*, here "worship."

272. Arcades: "Arcadians, people of Arcadia," a region of Greece in the central Peloponnnesus. Greek nominative plural (note scansion - uu).

plurimus: "most often present" (*OLD* 3).

273. testis erit . . . : i.e., the Arcadian places mentioned will be witnesses to the god's presence throughout the region.

Pholoe: nominative; a mountain.

Stymphalides: "of Stymphalus," a lake. Greek nominative (see on 272).

274. quique . . . Ladon = *et Ladon qui*.

Ladon: a river.

275. pinetis: < *pinetum*, "pine forest."

Nonacrini: "of Nonacris," a mountain; modifies *nemoris* (< *nemus*, "grove; forest"). Note the rare fifth-foot spondee, a phenomenon often produced by a Greek proper name.

276. Cyllene: feminine; a mountain.

Parrhasiae: "of Parrhasia," a town or district.

277. numen: here, "deity."

278. munus: i.e., "sacrifice."

ob: "in return for."

ferebat: See on 129.

279. Evander: legendary Arcadian hero who migrated to Italy, where he founded the city Pallanteum.

280. locus: "(only) the site."

Ovid, *Fasti II* 23

281. inde: "therefore."
deum = *Pana*.
sacra: "the rites (of Pan)," i.e., the Lupercalia.
Pelasgis: < *Pelasgi*, believed to be the oldest inhabitants of Greece; here and often = *Graeci*.
282. flamen ... Dialis: See on 21. This is a difficult line of uncertain text. Translate: "the flamen Dialis was (already) at these (rites) according to ancient custom" or "the flamen Dialis was (in attendance) until these times (and still is) according to ancient custom."
283-380. Four explanations why the Luperci run naked.
283. Note the word play with *cur* and forms of *curro*.
284. nuda ferant ... corpora: translate "run naked."
posita [= **deposita**, "taken off"] **... veste:** ablative absolute logically coordinate with *ferant;* translate "they take off their clothes and run naked."
285-288. First explanation: the god.
285. deus: Pan/Faunus.
velox: adjective with adverbial force; "quickly."
286. subitas concipit ... fugas: "takes suddenly to flight" (Frazer).
288. ad: "for"; the prepositional phrase is dependent upon *commoda* ("convenient, suitable").
289-302. Second explanation: the Arcadian heritage.
289. ante Iovem genitum: i.e., "before the birth of Jupiter." The main idea is contained in the participle, as in the famous expression *ab urbe condita*, "from the foundation of the city" (*AG* 497). According to one version, Jupiter was born in Arcadia.
genitum: < *gigno*, "beget, create."
terras: sc. *suas*.
290. luna: ablative of comparison.
prior: "older."
291. vita: sc. *eorum erat*.
feris = *vitae ferarum;* dative with *similis*.
nullos ... per usus: "without expert knowledge and/or practical experience" (*OLD* 6b and 7a).
agitata: < *agito*, here "spend, live."
292. expers: "without, free of" (+ genitive).
293. pro: "as, in place of."
norant = *noverant*, "they knew" (see on 83).
frugibus: < *fruges, -um*, "crops, grain."
294. nectar: predicative.
hausta: < *haurio*, "scoop up."

296. colentis: present participle of *colo* (here, "till, cultivate"): "farmer."
298. corpus amicta: direct object with a passive used like the Greek middle voice (see on 78), "having clothed (its own) body"; *amicta* < *amicio*. The point is that the sheep's wool was not used for human clothing.
299. Iove: See on 138.
    durabant: "endured (bad weather, etc.), lived."
    gerebant: here, "had."
300. docta: "taught"; i.e., "accustomed"; modifies *corpora* (299).
    graves: modifies both *imbres* and *Notos* (< *Notus,* "south wind").
301. detecti: < *detego,* "uncover"; = "the naked ones," i.e., the Luperci.
    referunt monumenta: "renew the memory" (Peter).
    vetusti: with *moris* (302).
302. opes: "resources" (< *ops*). Ovid means that the naked Luperci attest to the scant resources of the ancient Arcadians.
303-358. Third explanation: Faunus, Hercules and Omphale.
303. cur . . . Faunus: sc. a phrase meaning "to explain" governing the indirect question.
    fugiat: "avoids."
304. traditur: < *trado,* "hand down, relate."
    antiqui: transferred from *fabula* (see on 77).
305. forte: See on 247.
    comes: "companion, attendant"; goes closely with *ibat;* "in the company (of), in attendance (upon)."
    Tirynthius: "(the one) from Tiryns," a Greek town; i.e., Hercules. After he had killed Iphitus, the son of Eurytus of Oechalia, Hercules was told by Apollo that he could be purified of the crime if he were sold into slavery and the price given to Iphitus' father. The purchaser was the Lydian queen Omphale (here *dominae*).
306. excelso: "lofty" (< *excello,* "raise up").
307. incaluit: < *incalesco,* "grow warm/hot (here, with passion)."
    numina: vocative.
308. nil . . . est: See on 101. *nil = nihil.*
309. umeros perfusa: another object with a "middle" passive (see on 298), or else accusative of specification with a regular passive (see on 110). *perfusa* (< *perfundo*), "overspread."
310. Maeonis: "Lydian" (see on 120); i.e., Omphale. Nominative singular.

Ovid, *Fasti II* 25

aurato ... sinu: "(her) bosom decorated with gold"; ablative of specification.

conspicienda: gerundive of *conspicio:* "worthy to be looked at, distinguished."

311. umbracula: < *umbraculum,* "parasol"; poetic plural.

soles: < *sol;* the plural frequently = "light/heat of the sun" (*OLD* 4b).

312. Herculeae: See on 237.

313. Tmoli: < *Tmolus,* a Lydian mountain famous for its wines.

tenebat: "she reached."

314. Hesperos: "Hesperus," the evening star. Masculine nominative.

roscidus: "dew-damp."

315. antra: < *antrum,* "cave, grotto"; poetic plural.

subit: < *subeo,* "enter."

tofis laqueata: "panelled (on the ceiling) with tufa (volcanic rock)." The top of the grotto with its *tofus* and *pumex* is compared to the costly panelled ceilings (*laquearia*) found in elegant Roman buildings.

vivo: The rock is "living" in that it resides in its original location.

316. garrulus: "babbling."

in primo limine: "at the edge of the threshold."

317. parant: Historical present (see on 105) with the meaning of the imperfect is common after *dum.*

318. cultibus: < *cultus,* here "clothing, finery."

Alciden: Greek accusative of the patronymic *Alcides,* "grandson of Alceus," a common epithet of Hercules.

319. Gaetulo: "Gaetulian." The Gaetuli were a people of northwestern Africa.

murice tinctas: See on 107.

320. modo: See on 79.

cincta fuit: < *cingo.* For tense see on 176.

321. ventre: < *venter,* "belly"; i.e., of Hercules.

vinc(u)la relaxat: "undoes the fastenings."

322. posset: Subjunctive clauses depending upon verbs in the historical present follow either the primary or (as here) secondary sequence.

exseruisse: The perfect infinitive is sometimes used instead of the present to emphasize the completion of the action; in poetry the substitution is made more often for metrical convenience.

323. armillas: "bracelets."

        illa: with *bracchia*.
        ad: See on 288.
324. **scindebant:** "split."
        vincula: i.e., the straps on the shoes.
325. **ipsa** = *Omphale*, who puts on Hercules' clothing.
        clavam: the "club" always carried by Hercules.
        spoliumque leonis: i.e., the skin worn by Hercules that he had stripped from the Nemean lion in the first of his Labors.
326. **tela minora:** i.e., Hercules' arrows, smaller by comparison with the club.
        sua: "their"; refers to *pharetra*.
327. **sic:** i.e., in each other's clothing.
        functi: < *fungor*, here "enjoy" or "complete" (+ ablative).
328. **iuxta:** modifies *positis*.
        secubuere: < *secubo*, "sleep apart/alone."
329. **causa:** sc. *secubandi erat*.
        repertori: < *repertor*, "discoverer, inventor"; the god Bacchus.
330. **facerent:** subjunctive in a relative clause of purpose.
        pure: Sexual abstinence was demanded before the celebration of many religious rites.
        foret orta = *orta esset;* < *orior*, "rise, begin."
333. **comites:** the "attendants" outside the cave.
        solutos: "weakened, relaxed" (< *solvo*, "loosen").
334. **spem capit:** "he entertains/conceives the hope"; the verbal idea in *spem* is followed by indirect statement.
        dominis: Omphale and Hercules.
        esse: instead of *futurum esse* because the condition is imagined as already existing.
        soporis: < *sopor*, "sleep"; partitive genitive with *idem:* "the same sleep."
335. **huc illuc:** "to and fro, this way and that."
336. **cautas:** "cautious," an epithet transferred from the subject.
        subsequiturque: "and follows (them)."
337. **strati . . . cubilia lecti:** lit., "the couches of the bed spread out"; i.e., "the place where the beds were spread out." *strati:* < *sterno*.
        captata: < *capto*, "try to touch, grasp at."
338. **sorte:** < *sors* (feminine), "drawing of lots"; here "attempt."
        futurus erat: lit., "was about to be"; i.e., "would have been."

339. saetis: ablative of specification with *hirsuta:* "rough with bristles."
340. sustinuitque: "and pulled back."
341. rediit: The final syllable of the 3rd singular perfect of *eo* and its compounds is often long.
342. viso . . . angue: ablative of means or ablative absolute.
343. inde: See on 113.
   tori: genitive with *velamina*.
344. nota: "mark, sign"; i.e., of who was sleeping there.
345. spondaque sibi propiore: "and . . . on the bed closer to him."
346. cornu: ablative of comparison.
347. ora . . . ab ima: "from the bottommost edge/hem."
348. horrebant: "bristled."
   crura: < *crus,* "leg."
   pilis: < *pilus,* "hair."
349. cetera: accusative plural, object of *[Faunum] temptantem.*
350. ille = *Faunus;*
351. inclamat: "calls for."
352. ignibus: "torches," by synecdoche (see on 95); in ablative absolute with *inlatis* (< *infero*).
354. humo: < *humus* (feminine), "ground."
355. ridet: For singular subject with two verbs see on 135.
   qui . . . iacentem = [*ei*] *qui videre* [= *viderunt*] *iacentem* (sc. *Faunum*).
356. Lyda puella: "Lydian woman"; often *puella* = "a young woman"; in the context of love = "young woman as object of sexual interest" (*OLD*).
357. lusus: < *ludo,* here "deceive."
   lumina: "the eyes"; object of *fallentes.*
359-380. Fourth explanation: Romulus and Remus.
359. peregrinis: "foreign"; sc. *causis;* i.e., the Greek aetiologies given above.
   causas . . . Latinas: The plural looks ahead to both the story beginning in 360 and the explanation of the name Lupercal in 381ff.
360. suo: i.e., of its native land, Italy.
   currat: jussive subjunctive.
   equus: Ovid often pictures a poem in progress as a racing chariot.
361. cornipedi: < *cornipes,* "horn-footed, hoofed"; see on 268.
   caesa . . . capella: ablative absolute.

de: "according to."
363. veribus [< *veru*] transuta salignis: "stuck on willow spits" (Frazer).
364. parant: See on 317.
    medias ... vias: See on 164.
365. frater: Remus.
366. solibus et campo: hendiadys (see on 214), "the sunny field," probably the Campus Martius just outside of Rome, which was used for athletic and military exercises.
    corpora ... dabant: i.e., were exercising.
367. caestibus: < *caestus*, "boxing glove"; ablative of means, as are *iaculis* and *pondere*.
    misso: "hurled."
    pondere saxi: i.e., a rustic Italian equivalent to the Greek discus.
368. bracchia ... experienda dabant: "gave (their) arms to be tested" (see on 134); "they tested their arms."
    per lusus: "in sport."
369. excelso: "a height" (cf. 306).
370. A violent disruption of normal word order called hyperbaton, here suggestive of the speaker's excitement. The two vocatives go together; *praedones* ("robbers") is the subject.
371. longum erat: idiom, "it would have taken long."
    armari: "to arm themselves."
372. partibus: "directions."
    occursu praeda recepta [sc. est] Remi: "the booty was recovered by the meeting of Remus"; i.e., Remus encountered the robbers and recovered the property.
373. stridentia: < *strideo*, here "sizzle."
374. non ... edet: The subject is indefinite; = *nemo edet* (< *edo*, "eat").
375. dicta: "things said"; i.e., "what he had said."
    Fabii: the ancestors of the family that fought at the Cremera (cf. 195ff.). Ovid is here attempting to give an aetiology for the two traditional divisions of the Luperci priesthood, the Luperci Fabiani or Fabii and the Luperci Quinctiales or Quinctilii (cf. 378).
    inritus: here, "unsuccessful."
376. nuda: modifies both *mensas* and *ossa* (< *os*, "bone").
377. et: "but at the same time, and yet" (*OLD* 14).
    indoluit: < *indolesco*, "grieve, be distressed"; introduces indirect statement.
379. posito velamine: cf. 284.

currunt: sc. *Luperci.*
380. memorem: "mindful (of), commemorating"; sc. the successful event.
[id] quod bene cessit: subject of *habet.*
cessit: < *cedo,* here "result, turn out."
381-424. Etymologies of the Lupercalia and the Lupercal, the latter being the sacred spot at the foot of the Palatine Hill where the rites began.
381. quaeras: the (potential) subjunctive regularly follows *forsitan* ("perhaps"); originally the construction was an indirect question (*fors sit an,* "it would be a chance whether"); contrast the indicative in 97.
sit: "is (called)."
382. -ve: See on 230.
383. Silvia: also known as Rhea Silvia or Ilia, was raped by the god Mars and gave birth to the twins Romulus and Remus.
Vestalis: "a Vestal virgin, priestess of Vesta."
caelestia semina: "heavenly seeds"; i.e., children by a divine father.
partu: "in birth."
384. ediderat: < *edo,* "bring forth."
patruo: < *patruus,* "uncle," King Amulius, who had seized the throne of Alba Longa from her father Numitor. Alba Longa, 13 miles southeast of Rome, had been founded by Aeneas' son Ascanius.
386. facis: Ovid apostrophizes Amulius.
istis: "those whom *you* are destroying" (Hallam).
Romulus: predicate nominative.
alter: "one (of the two)."
387. iussa: object of both *peragunt* and *recusantes* (< *recuso,* "object to").
389. quem Tiberim: direct object and predicate accusative ("the Tiber river") after *reddidit* (390; "made, gave the name of"). The relative's gender is attracted to that of *Tiberim.*
Tiberinus: an early king of Alba Longa.
391. fora: the Forum Romanum, the center of civic activity in Rome, and the Forum Boarium, the ancient cattle market (and perhaps also the vegetable market, the Forum Holitorium), low-lying areas in central Rome drained by the main sewer, the Cloaca Maxima.
videres: potential subjunctive; "you might/would have seen."
392. quaque [= et ubi]: parallel to the *ubi*-clause in 391.
Maxime Circe: the Circus Maximus, the great race course in the valley between the Palatine and Aventine Hills.
393. venerunt: sc. *ministri* from 387 as subject.

394. **et:** "or" (*OLD* 13).
395. **quam:** "how."
396. **ex illis:** "of the two" (Frazer).
   iste: i.e., Romulus.
   vigoris: genitive of the whole with *plus*.
397. **genus:** here, "lineage."
398. **nescio quem:** "some"; modifies *deum*.
399. **si quis . . . deus:** "if some god . . . " (see on 147).
400. **praecipiti tempore:** "critical situation."
401. **si . . . egeret:** Ilia too was in danger from Amulius; *egeret* < *egeo*, "be in need of," + ablative.
   ope: ablative with *egeret* ("were in need of").
403. **nata:** < *nascor*, "be born"; with *corpora* in 404.
404. **corpora:** vocative. *Corpus* occasionally = "person."
   desierat [< *desino*, "cease"] **deposuitque:** parataxis with the former verb logically dependent upon the latter (see on 149-50); = *cum desiisset, deposuit* (*geminos*).
405. **vagierunt:** < *vagio*, "cry." The -e- in the 3rd plural perfect active ending is sometimes short.
   sensisse putares = [*eos*] *sensisse* [*verba ministri*] *putares:* "you would have thought that (they) had understood (the servant's words)." *putares:* see on 391.
406. **hi** = *ministri*.
   tecta: here, "houses."
   genis: < *gena*, "cheek."
407. **impositos:** "(the infants) put in (it)."
   summa . . . unda: "on the surface of the water."
   alveus: "a hollow, troughshaped vessel" (*OLD*); i.e., "ark" or "basket."
408. **fati:** genitive of the whole with *quantum*.
   tabella: here "board, plank," i.e., the *alveus*.
409. **in limo:** with *sedet* ("becomes lodged, sticks") in 410.
   silvis: dative with the compound *adpulsus*.
410. **paulatim:** modifies *deficiente* (here, "falling, receding"; in ablative absolute with *fluvio*).
411. **quaeque** = *et quae*.
412. **Rumina . . . ficus:** The usual title is *ficus Ruminalis*, the fig tree near the Lupercal sacred to the minor deity Rumina, who was probably associated with suckling (*rumis* = *mamma*, "breast").
   Romula = *Romulea*, "of Romulus."
413. **expositos:** "abandoned."
   mirum: "an astonishing event!"

feta: adjective; "having just given birth."
gemellos: diminutive of *geminos*. Besides denoting smallness, the diminutive is also often pathetic: "the poor little twins."
414. **credat:** deliberative subjunctive (see on 8).
non nocuisse feram: indirect statement after *credat;* *nocuisse* < *noceo,* "harm" (+ dative).
415 **parum est:** "it is not enough."
prodest: < *prosum,* "help."
quos: sc. *eos* as antecedent.
416. **cognatae:** "related"; i.e., "of their relatives."
sustinuere: here, "ventured, were cruel enough (to)."
417. **blanditur:** < *blandior,* "caress" (+ dative).
418. **fingit:** Animals were said to "form" their new born by licking them. Compare our expression "lick into shape."
bina = *duo.*
419. **Marte:** ablative of source or origin.
[eos] satos [esse]: < *sero* ("sow, plant"); "(they were) begotten."
ducunt: here, "suck."
420. **nec** = *et non;* the negative goes with *promissi,* "intended."
lactis: < *lac,* "milk."
421. **illa** = *lupa.*
loco: the Lupercal (see on 381-424).
422. **magna . . . praemia:** i.e., having the place and the festival named after her.
lactis: objective genitive with *praemia* ("reward [for]").
423-424. As an afterthought, Ovid suggests another derivation, this one Greek.
423. **Arcadio . . . monte:** The mountain in Arcadia is Lycaeus.
dictos [esse] . . . Lupercos: The accusative + infinitive is regular after *veto* ("forbid")
424. **Faunus [= Pan] . . . Lycaeus:** the epithet designates the god's place of worship, as often (cf. 69, 91).
425-452. The custom of the Luperci striking the women they meet with straps of hide.
425. **nupta:** "bride, wife."
pollentibus: < *pollens,* "powerful"; i.e., magical.
426. **carmine:** here, "incantation."
427-428. **excipe** ["accept, receive"] **. . . habebit:** See on 159-60.
427. **fecundae:** usually = "fruitful," but here "(the hand) making fruitful." The whipping was a fertility rite.

428. iam: "soon."
socer: "father-in-law."
429. dies: See on 58.
dura . . . sorte: ablative of cause.
cum: "when," + indicative.
430. uteri: genitive singular; see on 211.
pignora: < *pignus*, "pledge"; here, "love-pledges," i.e., children.
rara: translate as adverb.
431. quid . . . prodest: "what good is it?"
Sabinas: "the Sabine women" (see on 139).
432. hoc: nominative.
illo = *Romulo*.
fuit: here, "occurred" (*L&S* s.v. *sum*, I.2).
433. mea . . . iniuria: subject; Romulus refers to the Rape of the Sabines.
vires: "strength," i.e., through an increase in the population.
bellum: "(only) war," i.e., the conflict between the Romans and the Sabines following the Rape.
434. fuerat: "it would have been"; pluperfect indicative for subjunctive in contrary-to-fact condition with protasis implied from the previous sentence.
nurus: < *nurus*, properly "daughter-in-law"; here, "woman." Accusative plural.
435. monte . . . Esquilio: "the Esquiline Hill," the largest of Rome's seven hills.
multis . . . annis: ablative of time within which functioning like accusative of extent of time; goes with *incaeduus* ("uncut," an Ovidian neologism).
436. nomine: "with the name of"; i.e., dedicated to.
437. nuptaeque virique: "both wives and husbands."
438. posito . . . genu: "on bended knee."
439. cacumina: < *cacumen*, "top"; nominative; or perhaps accusative of specification (see on 110), with *silvae* as subject. The trembling of the landscape is frequently a sign of a deity's presence.
440. mira: "astonishing (words)"; neuter plural accusative.
locuta: sc. *est*.
441. matres: object of *inito*.
inito: < *ineo*; 3rd person future imperative, "let . . . go into." Ovid is etymologizing: one of Faunus' names was Inuus, "the fructifying god" (*L&S*).
442. obstipuit . . . sono: for the construction see on 91.

Ovid, *Fasti II* 33

       dubio: Divine utterance is regularly ambiguous.
443. **intercidit:** lit., "fell between"; "has been lost/forgotten."
444. **exul:** in apposition with subject of *venerat*.
       humo: here, "region."
445. **iussae:** i.e., by the seer.
446. **pellibus exsectis:** see on 31.
       percutienda: < *percutio*, "strike"; for the construction with *do* see on 134.
447. **decimo . . . motu:** "in its tenth movement"; i.e., the tenth month. See on 175.
449. **gratia:** sc. *est* or *sit*; "thanks."
       Lucinae: < *Lucina*, Roman goddess of childbirth, often identified with Juno; dative.
       haec . . . nomina: i.e., the name Lucina.
450. **lucis:** < *lux;* i.e., the light seen by a newborn child; life.
451. **precor:** "I pray" (parenthetical).
       gravidis . . . puellis: "pregnant women"; dative after *parce*.
       facilis: here, "gentle, kind."

453-456. Weather-sign.

453. **orta . . . fuerit:** sc. *cum*.
       credere: infinitive after *desine:* "stop trusting" (+ dative).
455. **flamina:** < *flamen*, "breeze."
       sex . . . diebus: See on 435.
456. **carceris Aeolii:** "of the Aeolian prison." Aeolus, king of the winds, is frequently pictured keeping his subjects imprisoned in a cave.

457-474. The Constellation Pisces ("The Fish").

457. **levis:** "light," probably with reference to the 'lightening' of his load as water poured from the "tilted vessel" (see on 145).
       obliqua . . . urna: ablative of description.
       subsedit: The constellation "has set."
458. **proximus . . . excipe:** i.e., the sun moves from Aquarius to Pisces. The two are neighboring constellations in the celestial belt known as the zodiac through which the sun seems to move each year.
       proximus: nominative instead of vocative, since the latter is rarely used predicatively.
459. **memorant:** See on 114.

459-460. iuncta ... signa: "as constellations joined together." The two fish are united by a long 'string' of stars.

461. Typhona: Greek accusative of *Typhon*, one of the mythological giants who once attacked the Olympian gods.

Dione: properly the mother of Venus; here and elsewhere = Venus. Nominative singular.

463. Euphraten: Greek accusative of *Euphrates*, the famous river in Mesopotamia.

comitata: "accompanied" (< *comito*), regularly followed by ablative of agent without *ab*.

Cupidine: < *Cupido*, "Cupid," son of Venus.

464. Palaestinae ... aquae: the Euphrates; *Palaestinae* = "Syrian" by synecdoche.

465. populus: "poplar tree" (here probably singular for plural).

cannae: < *canna*, "reed."

summa: < *summum*, "top, surface."

466. salices: < *salix*, "willow tree."

hos: Dione/Venus and Cupid.

quoque: i.e., like the *summa riparum* covered by poplar and reeds.

467. latet: sc. *Dione* as subject.

insonuit vento: "rustled in the wind" (Frazer).

469. nymphae: the nymphs dwelling in the river.

470. dis: < *deus;* dative plural.

471. nec mora: sc. *erat*.

subiere: "moved up underneath (the gods)."

472. quo: "which (deed)."

sidera: in apposition with subject of *habent;* or perhaps direct object with *munus* in apposition.

473. inde: See on 281.

nefas: sc. *esse* in indirect statement after *ducunt* ("consider").

genus hoc: i.e., *pisces*.

mensis: < *mensa*, "table."

474. Syri: "Syrians"; subject of both *ducunt* and *violant* (here, "pollute").

475-512. February 16-17. The Quirinalia, festival in honor of Quirinus, a god of Sabine origin whom the Romans identified with the deified Romulus.

475. lux = *dies*, i.e., February 16.

vacua: sc. *sacris;* "without festivals."

tertia: For the method of counting see on 149-50.
dicta [est]: "(has been) appointed/dedicated."
477. curis: predicate nominative after *est dicta*.
478. bellicus . . . deus: Romulus/Quirinus. Romulus was noted for his achievements in war.
a: Motion from, cause, and source (i.e., deriving his name from) are all relevant meanings here, with the second perhaps predominating.
479. sive: sc. *quod*.
Quirites: "Roman citizens." Apparently the word originally designated the inhabitants of the Sabine town Cures (cf. 480) and was adopted by the Romans after they united with the Sabine community in the time of Romulus
480. Cures: See on 135; accusative.
481. nam: follows logically from 476.
pater: Mars, the father of Romulus.
moenia: sc. *Romae*.
483. Iuppiter: vocative.
484. sanguinis: i.e., "son."
officio: here, "service"; ablative after *eget*.
485. intercidit: In poetry the indicative is often used after *quamvis*, "although."
alter: i.e., Remus.
487. Mars's quotation of Jupiter is at the same time Ovid's quotation of the archaic epic poet Ennius (*Annales* fragment 65 Vahlen).
caerula: adjective used substantively, "the blue expanse."
488. sint rata: "let . . . be valid/granted fulfillment."
489. adnuerat: < *adnuo*, "nod."
489-490. uterque . . . polus: "each of the two poles," i.e., the complete vault of the heavens.
490. movit: "shifted" (Frazer).
Atlas: one of the race of gods called the Titans who were vanquished by Jupiter and the Olympians. Jupiter ordered Atlas to support the sky on his shoulders for eternity.
491. Understand *quem* before *antiqui*.
Capreae . . . paludem: "the marsh of the she-goat," a site in the Campus Martius.
492. tuis: sc. *civibus;* apostrophe to Romulus.
iura dabas: "you were prescribing laws."
493. fugit: "disappears."
removent: i.e., "blot out, darken."
subeuntia: "rising."

495. hinc: "then, next."
tonat: impersonal; "it thunders."
missis . . . ignibus: "lightning bolts hurled," i.e., by Jupiter.
496. fit fuga: "flight occurs"; i.e., "the people flee."
patriis: < *patrius*, "of (his) father." Romulus departs in the chariot of Mars.
497. falsaeque: The adjective is transferred to *caedis* from *crimine*.
patres: "senators"; subject.
in crimine: sc. *erant;* idiom, "they stood charged with" (+ genitive).
498. haesisset: "would have stuck" (< *haereo*); see on 381.
animis: sc. *populi* or *civium*.
fides: "suspicion" (Frazer).
499. Longa . . . Alba: See on 384; ablative of place from which.
500. facis: < *fax, facis*, "torch."
usus: here, "need."
501. subito: adjective modifying *motu*.
saepes . . . sinistrae: "hedges on the left." In Roman augury omens appearing on the left were believed to be lucky.
502. horruerunt: < *horresco*, "bristle, stand on end." For the short -e- see on 405.
503. humano = *homine;* ablative of comparison with *maior*.
trabea: a toga decorated with scarlet stripes and a purple border, worn in classical times by the equites and said to have been the garb of the Roman kings. Ablative of specification.
504. visus [est]: "seemed, appeared."
505. dixisse: For tense see on 322.
lugere Quirites: accusative + infininitive after *prohibe:* "Prohibit the citizens from grieving."
506. numina nostra: "my divinity"; direct object.
507. placent: < *placo* (see on 33); plural after the collective subject *turba*.
508. patrias: "of (their) fathers, ancestral."
artes militiamque: hendiadys (see on 214).
509. iussit: sc. *sic*.
oculis: "from sight."
evanuit: < *evanesco*, "disappear."
510. hic: Proculus.
populos: poetic plural, as is *templa* in 511.
refert: See on 203.

511. collis ... dictus ab illo est: the Quirinal Hill, one of the seven hills of Rome.
512. certi: "fixed"; i.e., the Quirinalia was one of the *feriae statae* or *stativae* performed at the same time every year, as opposed to the moveable feasts (*feriae conceptivae*), whose dates were decided annually by priests or magistrates.
    sacra paterna: "the rites of (our fore-) fathers."

513-532. February 17. *Stultorum festa*, the last day of the Fornacalia.

513. lux: See on 475.
    festa: plural for singular.
514. accipe = *audi*.
515. tellus antiqua: translate "the earth in olden times."
    colonos: "farmers" or "inhabitants."
517. laudis: with *plus*.
518. domino: "the owner" of the field.
519. farra: See on 24.
    veteres: See on 22.
    iaciebant: here, "sowed."
520. primitias: "the first fruits"; in apposition with *farra resecta*.
    Cereri: < *Ceres*, goddess of grain.
521. usibus: "by (their) experience(s)." Latin often uses the plural where English prefers a collective singular.
    admoniti: < *admoneo*, here "teach, prompt."
    [farra] torrenda dederunt: The grain must be parched before it is pounded.
523-524. modo ... nunc: "now ... now, at one time ... at another."
523. verrebant: "they were sweeping up."
    pro: "instead of."
524. corripuere: < *corripio*, "seize, take hold of, attack."
525. Fornax: "oven, furnace." Subject.
    Fornace: ablative with *laetus*.
526. temperet: "manage/regulate" (the toasting of).
527-528. curio ... maximus: the head of the college of officials called *curiones*. Each *curio* was the leader of one of Rome's *curiae*, ancient divisions of the city's population.
527. legitimis ... verbis: "words prescribed by law"; i.e., established formulas.
528. indicit: < *indico*, "announce, give notice of."

38 Ovid, *Fasti II*

   nec: modifies *stata*, "fixed, appointed" (< *sisto*); see on 512.
529. **multa . . . tabella:** "many a tablet"; in ablative absolute with *pendente*.
530. **certa . . . nota:** "by a particular/fixed mark," i.e., on one of the tablets. Apparently each tablet marked the spot where a *curia* would gather for the announcement of the Fornacalia and perhaps also for the general celebration on the final day of the festival.
532. **relata:** either "assigned" (i.e., to the last day of the festival) or "repeated." Ovid seems to mean that the Fornacalia was observed at separate meetings of the *curiae* on different days, but that a person who did not know to which *curia* he belonged participated only in the general celebration on the last day of the festival.

533-616. February 21. The Feralia, the final day of the *dies parentales* or Parentalia in honor of the dead which began on February 13.

533. **animas:** "souls, spirits."
534. **exstinctas . . . pyras:** "extinguished pyres"; i.e., "tombs, graves."
535. **manes:** See on 52; nominative.
   pietas: "devotion (to family, gods, and state)."
   pro: See on 523.
   divite: < *dives*, "rich."
536. **Styx:** a river of the underworld; feminine.
   ima: "below, in the underworld."
537. **tegula:** "a (roof-)tile."
   porrectis . . . coronis: "with votive garlands"; *porrectis* < either *porricio*, "lay offerings before the gods" or *porrigo*, "extend, offer."
   satis est: predicate; singular verb with more than one subject; compound subject continues through line 539.
   velata: < *velo*, "cover, decorate."
538. **fruges:** "grain, meal."
539. **mero:** < *merum*, "wine."
   Ceres: "bread," by metonomy.
   solutae: "loose" (< *solvo*).
540. **haec:** accusative.
   testa = *tegula* (537).
   media . . . via: "in the middle of the road." Roman graves are frequently located on the sides of the roads outside of the city.
541. **maiora:** sc. *munera*.

542. positis ... focis: "at the (sacrificial) hearths set up (by you)."
  sua: here, "due, appropriate, proper" (*OLD* B.12); i.e., to either the shades, the hearths, or the situation.
543. pietatis idoneus auctor: "a suitable authority on devotion." In Virgil's *Aeneid, pius* is the hero's regular epithet.
544. terras ... tuas: i.e., Latium. Ovid apostrophizes the eponymous king of the region.
545. patris: Anchises. In *Aeneid* 5 Aeneas celebrates the anniversary of his father's death with games at his burial place in Sicily, and he promises to observe the day always.
  genio: < *genius*, the tutelary spirit of an individual or a family; here = *umbra* or *manes*.
  sollemnia: The meanings "annual" and "solemn" are both appropriate to the context.
546. hinc: "from this (example)."
  edidicere: < *edisco*, "learn thoroughly."
547. gerunt: sc. *Romani* as subject.
548. deseruere: < *desero*, "neglect."
549. impune fuit: < *impune est*, "go unpunished."
  omine ab isto: "after that (ill-)omen(-ed event)."
550. suburbanis: adjective, "near the city." The burning and burial of the dead took place outside of the city.
  incaluisse: See on 307.
551. bustis: < *bustum*, "tomb"; ablative of place from which.
  exisse: See on 203.
552. questi [esse]: < *queror*, "complain, lament." The subject is *avi*, "ancestors," i.e., "ghosts of our ancestors."
553. ululasse = *ululavisse*, < *ululo*, "shriek, howl."
554. deformes animas: "disfigured spirits"; subject of *ululasse* in indirect statement.
  inane: "insubstantial."
555. praeteriti: "neglected" (< *praetereo*, "pass by").
556. prodigiis: < *prodigium*, "portent"; happenings like those of 551-54.
  modus: "moderation, a limit."
557. viduae: "without husbands."
  cessate: "wait"; i.e., "do not marry."
558. exspectet: jussive subjuctive, as is *comat* (560).
  pinea taeda: The "pine torch" was a regular feature of marriage celebrations.
559. tibi: dative of reference.

cupidae: "eager (for your marriage)."
videbere = *videberis*.
560. hasta: As part of the Roman pre-nuptial ritual, the bride's hair was parted or combed with a spear.
561. Hymenaee: Hymenaeus was the god of marriage; vocative.
ignibus atris: "the smoky (or gloomy) fires"; apparently referring to the torches carried in a funeral procession and held at the burial, or else to the funeral pyre itself.
563. I.e., the temples must remain closed on this day, so that the spirits of the dead will not pollute them--the same reason for the prohibition against marriage.
565. tenues: "insubstantial."
functa: See on 327.
566. cibo: ablative with *pascitur* ("feeds on"); the ritual meal left at the grave.
567-568. "Yet these (rites) are not (held) longer than (the time when) as many days of the month are left as my (elegiac) poems have feet"; i.e., the Parentalia end eleven days before the end of the month, i.e., on the 18th. But Ovid's dating is wrong, since the last day was February 21.
tot . . . quot: "as many . . . as."
567. supersint: *quam* after a comparative sometimes introduces a subjunctive clause, usually with an accompanying relative pronoun or *ut*.
568. Luciferi = *dies*.
quot . . . pedes: The Romans considered the elegiac couplet to have eleven feet.
569. iusta: "funeral offerings" (*OLD* 3b).
ferunt . . . Feralia: Ovid makes explicit the etymology he has already hinted at (534; 545).
570. placandis manibus: dative; = *placando manes* (see on 18).

571-616. The rites of the obscure goddess *Tacita* ("the Silent Goddess"), magical rites which are not part of the official Roman religion.

571. anus: "old woman" (fourth declension).
annosa: "aged, old."
572. Tacitae: sc. *deae*.
ipsa = *anus*.

573. tria tura: "three portions of incense." The number three occurs frequently in connection with rituals, especially those of a magical sort.
574. qua: "where."
575. cantata: "enchanted, charmed" (< *canto*, "sing"). I.e., a spell had been chanted over the threads.
576. septem: another magic number.
577. quodque . . . quod: Both relatives have *caput* in 578 as antecedent.
    pice: < *pix, picis*, "pitch."
    adstrinxit: < *adstringo*, "fasten, bind."
    acu . . . aena: "a bronze needle." *aena:* trisyllabic.
578. obsutum: < *obsuo*, "sew up."
    maenae: < *maena*, a small fish. Fish were proverbial for their silence.
579. instillat: "she pours on drop by drop"; sc. *capiti maenae*.
    vini quodcumque: "whatever wine."
581. vinximus: < *vincio*, "bind." The purpose of the rite was to silence enemies. Thus is the deity's name explained.
583-616. Ovid explains the identity of the Silent Goddess.
583. dea Muta = *dea Tacita*.
584. per antiquos . . . senes: The person through whom or by means of whom something is done is regularly expressed by *per* + accusative. The phrase belongs in the indirect question *quae . . . nota* [*sint*].
585. Iuturnae: Juturna was an old Italian water-deity; objective genitive after *amore*.
586. multa tulit . . . non patienda: "endured many things that ought not to be suffered."
587. illa = *Iuturna*.
587-588. modo . . . nunc: See on 523-24.
587. coryleta: "hazel thickets."
588. cognatas: "related (to her)."
589. hic = *Iuppiter*.
    quaecumque tenebant: "all those who were dwelling in."
590. iacit: here, "throws off, utters" (*OLD* 8).
    choro: See on 156.
591. Translate: "She begrudges to herself (and avoids) what is expedient for her."
    invidet: < *invideo*, "begrudge" (+ dative of the person [*sibi*] and accusative of the thing).

592. concubuisse: < *concumbo*, "lie with" (+ dative); in apposition with *quod expedit illi* (591).
593. consulite: < *consulo*, here "have regard for, be mindful of" (+ dative).
  quae: sc. *erit*.
595. illi = *Iuturnae*.
  in prima ... ripa: "on the edge of the bank."
  obsistite: < *obsisto*, "stand in the way of, impede" (+ dative).
596. sua ... corpora = *se*.
597. Tiberinides: "of the river Tiber" or (as patronymic) "daughters of the river-god Tiber"; an Ovidian neologism found only here; scanned uu-uu.
598. quaeque = *et omnes nymphae quae*.
  colunt: here, "inhabit."
  Ilia: See on 383. After the birth of Romulus and Remus, Amulius had Ilia thrown into the Tiber (in some accounts the Anio), where the river-god took her (now a deity) as his wife.
599. nais: "a water nymph, naiad"; nominative singular; disyllabic.
599-601. prima sed ... positum = *sed illi nomen antiquum, ex vitio positum, erat prima syllaba bis dicta* (i.e., *Lala*).
601. vitio [suo]: Her "defect" or "failing" was chattering, *lalein* in Greek.
  positum: here, "given."
  Almo: a river which flows into the Tiber; here the river-god and father of Lara. Nominative singular.
603. quae simul ac: "as soon as she"; for the relative see on 173.
605. miserata: < *miseror*, "pity, lament."
606. naida: Greek accusative of *nais*.
607. intumuit: < *intumesco*, "swell up (with anger), fly into a rage."
  quaque = *et qua;* ablative with *usa* (< *utor*, "use").
608. huic = *Larae;* dative of separation, regularly used (especially of persons) instead of the ablative after verbs compounded with *ab-, de-, ex-* and (less frequently) *ad-*.
  Mercurium: < *Mercurius*, the god Mercury, one of whose functions was to escort souls of the dead to the Underworld.
609. manes: here, "the Underworld."
  silentibus: The dead were often called *silentes*.
610. nympha: sc. *erit*, or perhaps *est*.
611. euntes: i.e., Mercury and Lara on their way to the Underworld.

612. illa = *Lara*.
   placuisse: < *placeo*, "please" (+ dative); i.e., "to have attracted the attention of."
613. parat: "intends" (*OLD* 8).
614. nititur: < *nitor*, "struggle, make an effort."
615. gravis = *gravidus*, "pregnant."
   parit: < *pario*, "give birth to."
   compita: "crossroads."
616. vigilant: "keep watch."
   Lares: Roman deities who guarded the home, the crossroads and the city (respectively, the *Lares familiares, compitales* and *praestites*); in apposition with *geminos* in 615 but placed in emphatic final position as a sort of punch line: Lara was the mother of the Lares.

617-638. February 22. Caristia or Cara Cognatio, a private family celebration.

617. Proxima: sc. *sacra*.
   cognati . . . cari: "dear relatives"; *Caristia* < Greek *charisteia*, "thank offerings." Ovid suggests a (false) derivation from *carus*.
618. socios . . . deos: "the gods shared (by members of the family)"; i.e., the Penates and Lar familiaris.
   turba propinqua = *turba propinquorum*, "a crowd of kinsmen."
619. qui: antecedent is *propinquis*.
620. ora referre: "to bring back (one's/our) gaze," i.e., thoughts.
   iuvat: impersonal; "it is pleasing" (+ infinitive).
621. postque tot amissos: See on 289.
   quicquid . . . restat: object of *aspicere* (622).
   sanguine: i.e., "family."
622. generis . . . gradus: either "stages of the family" (i.e., generations) or "degrees of relationship."
623. innocui veniant: "let (only) the innocent come"; a demand for ritual purity.
   procul hinc, procul impius esto: version of the ritual formula whereby the officiant at a celebration warded off the profane. *Procul* is repeated for emphasis: "Far from here, far away let the wicked (brother) be." *esto* < *sum;* 3rd person future imperative.
624. in partus . . . suos: "towards her children."
625-626. Each clause refers to a different offender.

625. cui: dative of reference.
vivax: "living (too) long"; i.e., he cannot wait until his father dies.
digerit: here, "counts" (*OLD* 4c).
626. premit: "torments."
socrus: "mother-in-law."
627. Tantalidae: nominative plural; "the grandsons of Tantalus," i.e., Thyestes, who seduced his brother's wife, and the brother Atreus, who murdered Thyestes' children and served them to him as a meal.
Iasonis: < *Iason*, "Jason," leader of the Argonauts and husband of Medea (see on 42).
628. semina tosta: Ino distributed "toasted seeds" among the farmers of Boeotia as part of an intrigue against her step-children Phrixus and Helle. When the seeds did not grow and the oracle at Delphi was consulted, Ino bribed the messengers to say that the god demanded the sacrifice of the children.
629. soror: Philomela, sister of Tereus' wife Procne. Tereus seduced (or raped) his sister-in-law and cut out her tongue to prevent her from telling. Procne (or Philomela) took revenge by serving Tereus his son as a meal. All three were then transformed into birds.
631. dis generis: "the gods of the family," the Lares (cf. 634) and/or the ancestral spirits.
boni = the *innocui* of 623; vocative.
Concordia: the goddess Concord.
632. praecipue: "especially"; probably modifies *illa die* rather than *mitis*.
633. libate: < *libo*, here "offer/dedicate (to the gods)."
grati pignus honoris: "as a pledge of the homage pleasing (to these gods)"; in apposition with *patella*, "plate (of offerings)" in 634.
634. incinctos = *succinctos*, "girded up, with (their) tunics gathered up," as the Lares are often represented in art.
missa: here, "offered."
636. larga ... vina: "much wine"; i.e., cups brimming with wine.
precaturi: The future active participle sometimes expresses purpose; "to pray."
637. bene vos, bene te: an idiom for toasts; "good health to you" (sc. *valere volumus* or some such phrase).
vos = *Lares*.
pater patriae: cf. 119ff. The title is especially appropriate in the context of a family festival.

Caesar: Augustus, whose *genius* (see on 545) was represented with the Lares at the crossroads, and in whose honor libations were poured at public and private banquets after a senate decree of 30 B.C.

638. suffuso ... mero: ablative absolute; "while the libation is poured."

sint: jussive.

639-684. February 23. Terminalia.

640. Construe: *deus qui arva indicio suo separat. deus:* subject of *celebretur* (639).

separat: "divides," i.e., establishes the boundaries of.

indicio: < *indicium*, "mark, symbol."

641. Termine: See on 50.

sive ... sive: Prayers and hymns frequently use this construction to note a deity's various names, powers, or (as here) manifestations.

lapis: sc. *es*.

defossus: < *defodio*, "bury"; here, "set (in the ground)."

642-644. tu ... te ... tibi: Repetition of the second person pronoun is a characteristic of hymns and prayers (cf. below 659-63).

642. stipes: "post"; nominative.

ab: "from the time of."

habes: With expressions of duration of time (here *ab antiquis*) the present tense denotes an action begun in the past and continuing in the present.

643. diversa ... de parte: "from/on opposite sides."

644. bina: See on 418.

liba: < *libum*, "sacrificial cake."

645. curto ... testu: "in a broken pot" or "on a broken piece of pottery."

646. colona: "farmer's wife."

647. minuit: "makes small"; i.e., "chops."

concisa: < *concido*, "cut"; sc. *ligna*.

arte: "skillfully."

648. pugnat: here, "strives, takes pains." The branches are stuck in the ground to support the pile of logs.

649. inritat: "kindles."

cortice: < *cortex*, "bark."

650. puer: often = "slave," but here "young son."

651. inde: "from these (baskets)."

ter: Many ritual actions must be performed "three times" (cf. 573 and 575).

652. incisos: < *incido*, "cut up."

653. libantur singula [vina]: "(a portion of) each (container of) wine is poured as a libation."

654. linguis . . . favet: a religious formula, "shows favor with (their) tongues"; i.e., "keeps silent (in order to avoid words of bad omen)."

candida: "(clad in) white." Participants in a religious celebration regularly wore white garments.

655. communis: "common (to both properties)."

Terminus: i.e., the boundary stone or post representing the god.

656. lactans: "unweaned, sucking."

657. vicinia: "neighborhood"; the collective subject takes plural verbs.

simplex: "ingenuous, unaffected."

659-678. A poetic version of the *laudes* (658) sung in the god's honor.

659. finis: < *finio*, "mark the boundaries of."

660. litigiosus: "contested."

661. ambitio: "partiality, favoritism" (Peter) or "desire for advancement, ambition" (*OLD* 4a).

662. legitima . . . fide: "in loyal good faith" (Frazer).

credita: "entrusted (to you)."

663. si tu signasses: "if you had marked the boundaries of."

Thyreatida: accusative of *Thyreatis*, "Thyreatic, pertaining to Thyrea," a disputed district on the border of Laconia and the Argolid in Greece. The chief cities Sparta and Argos agreed to a contest of 300 soldiers from each side as a means of settling the dispute. All perished except one Spartan and two Argives, who afterwards quickly returned to their native city.

664. leto: < *letum*, "death."

665. Othryades: the sole surviving Spartan warrior, who heaped up the enemy shields as a victory trophy, and on them painted his name with his own blood. Thus "(the name of) Othryades" was "read" on the pile of shields.

666. ille: Othryades.

dedit: either "gave," with the blood understood to be his own, or "caused, brought about (for)," with reference to the subsequent bloody argument over which side had won the contest.

667. quid: sc. *factum est* ("happened").

Capitolia: the Temple of Jupiter Optimus Maximus on the Capitoline Hill, which was said to have been built during the reign of Tarquinius Superbus, Rome's last king.

667-668. deorum cuncta ... turba: i.e., all the gods with shrines already on the hill.

668. cessit: < *cedo,* "yield"; i.e., the gods agreed to the project by granting favorable auspices.

669. inventus: "where he was found" (Frazer).

670. restitit: < either *resto* or *resisto;* "remained."

671. se supra = *supra se;* belongs in the *ne*-clause.

   cernat: sc. *Terminus* as subject.

672. tecta: "roof"; subject.

673. levitas: "mobility" (*L & S*); "desire for movement, restlessness" (*OLD* 1b); "want of steadfastness" (Hallam).

674. qua: modifies *statione.*

   positus fueris: future perfect; the long final syllable is archaic, sometimes preserved in poetry for metrical reasons.

676. Iovi: i.e., the god to whom you did not yield on the Capitoline.

678. clamato: 2nd person future imperative.

679. via: i.e., the via Laurentina, the road to Laurentum (see on 231). From the private rites described in 643ff. Ovid moves here to a public state sacrifice to Terminus.

   Laurentes ... agros: "the territory around Laurentum."

680. Dardanio ... duci: "Dardanian (= Trojan) leader," i.e., Aeneas, who landed in Laurentum and founded the town Lavinium nearby. Dardanus was a legendary ancestor of the Trojans.

   regna: in apposition with *Laurentes ... agros* (679).

681. illa: sc. *via;* ablative of place where.

   pecoris: here, "a sheep."

   fibris: "entrails," which were frequently sacrificed to the gods (cf. *exta,* 364); ablative of means.

682. sacra: here, "sacrifice"; subject of *fieri* after *videt.*

   sextus ... lapis: "the sixth mile-stone," an ancient boundary of the city of Rome; subject of *videt.*

683. limite certo: "with a fixed boundary"; ablative of description.

684. orbis: See on 130; genitive.

685-852. February 24. The Regifugium, a festival which Ovid and other authorities (probably falsely) interpreted as the commemoration of the flight of Tarquinius Superbus, the last king of Rome, from the city

(regis fuga, 685). Ovid adapts the historian Livy's narrative (1.53ff.) of the events leading up to the expulsion of Tarquin and his family.
685. **traxit:** "has derived" (< *traho*, "drag, draw").
illa = *regis fuga*.
686. **sextus . . . dies:** By Roman reckoning, 6 days from the end of February would be the 23rd, not the 24th. Ovid here seems to be offering an unexact variant of the standard way of designating February 24, *a(nte) d(iem) VI Kalendas Martias* ("six days before the first of March"), or perhaps he is thinking of a leap year, in which February has 29 days.
extremo: "the end of."
nomina: i.e., *Regifugium*.
687-688. **ultima . . . habebat regna:** "held the final kingly rule"; "was ruling as the final king."
687. **gentis:** objective genitive with *regna* (688).
688. **ad:** "with respect to."
689. **alias, alias:** "some . . . other."
690. **Gabios:** < *Gabii*, a city in Latium about 12 miles from Rome.
691. **trium minimus:** "the youngest of the three (sons)"; = Sextus Tarquinius.
manifesta: translate as adverb, "unmistakeably, plainly."
693. **nudaverant:** < *nudo*, here "unsheathe"; sc. *hostes* as subject.
694. **cupiant:** "(they) would wish"; potential subjunctive.
699. **ut . . . bella:** noun clause after *precantur*.
tueatur: here, "attend to."
700. **ignaris:** "unsuspecting" (< *ignarus*).
701. **potens:** "in charge."
misso . . . amico: ablative absolute.
702. **quod . . . monstret iter:** "what way he might show"; indirect question introduced by *appellat* ("appeals to, calls on") in 701, which contains an implicit idea of asking.
703. **odoratis . . . herbis:** ablative of specification with *cultissimus* ("very well cultivated").
suberat: "was below (his father's palace)."
704. **sectus humum rivo:** "its ground cut/divided by a stream." Properly *sectus* modifies *hortus* (703) and *humum* is accusative of specification (see on 110).
lene: adverbial accusative (= *leniter*).
706. **summa:** "the tops of."
metit: "cuts off, crops."

707. **decussa:** < *decutio*, "strike down, chop off."
708. **agnosco:** "I understand."
709. **principibus:** "chief citizens"; in ablative absolute with *caesis*.
   ex urbe Gabina: with *principibus*. *Ex* or *de* + ablative is occasionally used instead of the genitive after certain words, as it is regularly used after cardinal numbers. *Gabina:* "of Gabii."
710. **ducibus . . . suis:** ablative with *nuda* ("lacking the protection [of]").
711. **nefas visu:** "a dreadful thing to look at"; an interjection. *visu* is the supine in -*u*, sometimes used with *nefas* and other nouns, but more often with adjectives.
   mediis altaribus: "from between the altars" (Frazer). Ovid's elliptical narrative differs from the traditional account. The scene has shifted to Rome; in Livy the snake appears in the palace, and Tarquinius Superbus sends his sons Arruns and Titus (who take Brutus along) to Delphi, while Ovid seems to have a larger contingent in mind (*turba*, 716).
713. **consulitur Phoebus:** i.e., the oracle of Apollo at Delphi is asked the meaning of the prodigy of the snake.
   sors: here, "oracular response."
714. **princeps** = *primus*.
   victor: i.e., the next ruler of Rome.
715. **quisque:** "each" of the messengers sent to the oracle. The indefinite subject takes a plural verb, *tulerunt*.
716. **intellecto . . . deo:** ablative absolute or dative with *credula* ("trustful of").
   turba: in apposition with *quisque*.
717. **Brutus:** Lucius Junius Brutus, nephew of Tarquinius Superbus.
   stulti . . . imitator: Brutus played the fool by pretending to be a half-wit; *brutus* = "stupid." The juxtaposition of *stulti* and *sapiens* is an example of the rhetorical figure oxymoron (the combination of contradictory words).
719. **matri . . . Terrae:** The goddess Earth is frequently called *Mater*.
720. **offenso . . . pede:** "his foot having been knocked (against something)," i.e., "having tripped." Ablative absolute.
721. **Ardea:** nominative singular; a city in Latium some 20 miles south of Rome.
   signis: the military "standards" which designated sections of an army.

722. **patitur ... moras:** "endures long periods in a siege"; i.e., "endures a long, drawn-out siege."
723. **vacat:** impersonal; "there is time/leisure."
committere pugnam: "to engage in battle"; idiomatic.
724. **luditur:** impersonal passive; i.e., "they have fun."
otia ... agit: "spend (their) leisure."
miles: See on 199.
725. **Tarquinius iuvenis:** Sextus Tarquinius.
socios: "comrades."
726. **accipit:** "welcomes, entertains" (+ ablative of means).
ex: "among."
rege creatus: "the king's son"; *creatus = procreatus, natus.* *rege* is ablative of source or origin.
727. **sollicitos:** "restless."
728. **ad patrios ... deos:** i.e., home.
729. **ecquid:** interrogative particle; "Is it true that?"
in officio ... est: idiomatic, "is faithful to (its) allegiance" (*OLD* 3b).
torus ... socialis: "conjugal bed," i.e., the symbolic marriage bed located in the main hall of a Roman home, usually called the *lectus genialis*.
730. **mutua cura:** predicate nominative; i.e., do they care for us as much as we do for them?
731. **suam:** sc. *uxorem*.
studiis: < *studium*, "eagerness" or "devotion, partisanship." Ablative of means or cause.
certamina: "disputes."
733. **cui:** antecedent is understood subject of *surgit*.
Collatia: a town in Latium 10 miles east of Rome, by this time under Roman control.
nomen: His name was Lucius Tarquinius Collatinus.
734. **opus est:** idiom; "there is need (of)" (+ ablative).
735. **nox superest:** "there is night enough left"; i.e., there is enough time before dawn.
tollamur: "let us mount"; passive with reflexive force.
736. **frenis impediuntur:** "are bound with bridles, are bridled."
737. **pertulerant:** < *perfero*, "carry to one's destination."
illi: the *domini*.
738. **in fore:** "at the doorway."
739-740. **nurus ... pervigilare:** indirect statement after *inveniunt*.

739. fusis ... coronis: "with garlands spread over their necks"; the garlands regularly worn at parties had fallen from head to neck in the course of the festivities.

740. posito ... mero: "wine having been set down (before them)." Ablative absolute.

741. Lucretia: the wife of Collatinus. The scene now shifts to Collatia.

nebat: < *neo*, "spin, weave." Lucretia was engaged in the characteristic activity of the virtuous woman.

742. torum: the *lectus genialis* (see on 729).

calathi lanaque mollis: "baskets of soft wool"; hendiadys (see on 214).

743. ad: "by," governing *lumen ... exiguum*.

pensa: < *pensum*, "allotment of wool."

trahebant: "were drawing out," i.e., spinning. They drew out the woolen threads from the spindle.

745. domino = *ad Collatinum*. The dative is commonly found for *in/ad* + accusative in poetry.

746. quam primum: "as soon as possible."

lacerna: "military cloak"; an anachronism, since the *lacerna* was not introduced until much later in the Republic.

747. plura: sc. "than I can." Lucretia leads a sheltered life at home.

748. de bello: "of the war" (see on 709).

esse super = *superesse*, "to remain/be left."

749. victa cades: Lucretia apostrophizes Ardea.

melioribus: "(men) better (than yours are)."

restas: here, "resist" (+ dative).

751. sint tantum reduces: "if only they were returning!" *sint* is subjunctive expressing a wish.

sed enim: "but in fact."

temerarius: "rash"; predicate adjective.

752. qualibet: "wherever he pleases, everywhere."

753. mens abit: "my mind fails me."

morior: hyperbolic; i.e., "I faint."

pugnantis: sc. *mei coniugis*.

754. subit: "suggests itself to, comes over."

755. desinit in: "she leaves off/ends in."

remittit: "lets go, drops."

756. deposuitque: *-que* is postponed from the beginning of the line.

757. hoc: the action described in 756.

decuit: See on 106.

758. animo: ablative with both *digna* and *par*, although *par* regularly takes the dative.
759. revixit: < *revivesco*, "revive."
760. dulce . . . onus: in apposition with the subject.
761. iuvenis . . . regius = *Sextus*.
761-762. furiales . . . ignis concipit: *concipere ignem* = "to catch fire"; translate: "he burns furiously (with love), falls madly in love."
762. caeco: "blinding" or "hidden." Both meanings are apposite.
763. niveusque color: sc. of her skin, a light complexion being admired by the Romans, as was blond hair.
764. quique . . . decor = *et decor* ("charm, beauty") *qui*.
ab: "as a result of."
765. quod corrumpere non est: either "(that) which it is not possible to ruin," i.e., her chaste modesty, or "the fact that it is not possible to corrupt (her)," i.e., her incorruptibility. *Est* + infinitive = "it is possible (to)" (*L&S* I.B.5.b.e; *OLD* 9).
766. quoque minor . . . hoc magis: "and the less . . . the more"; correlative ablatives of degree of difference, a common construction.
767. dederat cantus: "had given (out its) songs"; i.e., "had crowed."
768. referunt . . . pedem: unspecific, "return"; remember that they were travelling by horse.
769. carpitur [< *carpo*, here "consume"] **adtonitos . . . sensus:** see on 309.
absentis: genitive.
770. ille = *Sextus*.
recordanti: < *recordor*, "recollect"; modifies understood *ei* following *placent*.
plura magisque placent: "more things please him, and please him more" (Hallam).
771-774. Ovid describes Tarquin's recollections in detail.
771. culta fuit: < *colo*, here "dress, adorn."
stamina: < *stamen*, "thread."
773. illi: dative of possession.
775. a: "after."
flatu: "blast of wind, gale."
776. a: "after and because of" (*OLD* 14).
777. aberat . . . praesentia: oxymoron (see on 717).
778. quem: The antecedent is *amor*.
praesens: "while (it was) present."

779. **ardet:** sc. *Sextus.*
780. **indigno:** "undeserving," i.e., of *vis* and *dolus*; dative modifying *toro.*
781. **exitus:** "outcome."
781-783. **audebimus . . . audentes . . . audendo:** The key concept is repeated, each time with a different form of the word (polyptoton).
781. **ultima:** "the utmost."
782. **viderit:** either jussive perfect subjunctive, "let her look out (for what's coming)" or future perfect indicative, "she will have seen (what I have planned)."
audentes . . . iuvat: proverbial.
783. **fatuoi** < *for,* "speak, say."
784. **latus:** < *latus, lateris.*
785. **aerata . . . porta:** "with her bronze gate"; ablative of description.
786. **condere:** "to hide," dependent on *parante.* The image both designates the time as just before sunset and suggests a response by nature to Sextus' imminent crime.
787. **ut:** "as, in the guise of."
penetralia: "home"; accusative.
Collatini: Note the rare spondee in the fifth foot (cf. 275).
788. **excipitur:** "is received/welcomed."
sanguine iunctus erat: Tarquinius Collatinus and Sextus Tarquinius were cousins.
789. **animis:** sc. *Lucretiae;* dative after the compound *inest.*
inscia rerum: "unaware of the facts."
791. **functus erat dapibus:** See on 327.
sua: "appropriate," i.e., for sleeping. See on 542.
792. **tota:** modifies the ablative *domo.*
795. **pressit:** "put his weight on."
mecum = *in mea manu.*
796. **natus . . . loquor:** "And this is the king's son Tarquin speaking."
797. **illa:** sc. *dixit.*
797-798. **neque enim . . . -que . . . aut:** "for . . . neither . . . nor . . . nor . . ."
798. **aliquid . . . mentis:** "any thought."
799. **quondam:** here, "sometimes."
stabulis . . . relictis: ablative absolute; "the stalls having been left"; i.e., it has strayed from the fold.
deprensa: < *depr[eh]endo,* "catch, find."

800. cum: belongs immediately after *ut* (799): "just as when . . ."
801. faciat: deliberative subjunctive (see on 229), as are *pugnet, clamet* (802) and *effugiat* (803).
   femina: general; "a woman."
802. qui vetet: sc. *eam clamare;* subjunctive in a relative clause of purpose: "to prevent (her from crying)." A rare use of the present subjunctive after a secondary tense.
804. externa: here, "belonging to someone unfamiliar" (*OLD* 3c); "of a stranger."
805. instat: sc. *eam;* "he urges (her)."
   amans hostis: oxymoron.
   pretioque: "and with a bribe."
807. nil agis: "you achieve nothing"; "it's no use" (*OLD* s.v. *ago* 21d).
   eripiam . . . vitam: unclear whether Sextus here means that he will kill her (sc. *tibi*) or the slave mentioned in 809 ("I will take away a life").
   per crimina: "with the accompaniment of accusations" (Hallam).
808. adulter: concessive; "though an adulterer (myself)."
809. deprensa: sc. *esse.*
810. famae: objective genitive with *metu:* "fear for (her) good name."
811. quid: "why?"
812. quanto: ablative of price.
   regnis . . . tuis: dative of reference.
   stetit: *stare* + ablative or genitive = "stand at the price (of), cost."
813. passis: "disheveled" (< *pando,* "spread out"); a sign of sorrow.
815. patrem: Spurius Lucretius Tricipitinus.
816. posita . . . mora: ablative absolute; = *sine mora.*
817. habitum: < *habitus,* "condition"; sc. *Lucretiae.*
   quae . . . causa: sc. *sit;* first of three indirect questions after *requirunt.*
818. -ve: See on 230.
819. pudibunda: "shamefaced."
820. more: "in the manner (of)."
821. hinc . . . hinc: "on this side . . . on that."
   solantur: < *solor,* "console, soothe." The (historical) present here is conative: "they try to soothe."
822. [ut] indicet: "(that) she reveal (what has happened)"; noun clause after *orant.*

823. ausa: < *audeo;* sc. *loqui.*
quarto: with *ausa.*
824. ideo: "for that reason"; i.e., in order to speak.
sustulit: < *tollo,* "raise."
825. hoc: direct object; explained in the next sentence.
eloquar: deliberative subjunctive.
827. restabant ultima: "the last part remained (unsaid)."
829. coactae [< *cogo,* "coerce"]: i.e., Lucretia; dative, or genitive with *facto* ("deed").
830. quam ... datis = *veniam quam ... datis.*
831. fixit: < *figo,* "pierce."
832. in patrios ... pedes: "at (her) father's feet."
833. ne ... honeste: noun clause after *respicit* ("takes care") in 834.
non ... honeste: "indecently"; i.e., uncovering her body.
834. haec ... cura: i.e., the care for decency.
836. decoris: < *decus,* "dignity, decorum"; genitive with *obliti* (< *obliviscor,* "forget").
837. Brutus: See on 717.
animo: here, "courage."
fallit: "proves false, belies."
838. semianimi: "half-alive"; ablative. The first *-i-* is treated as a consonant (synaeresis).
839. generoso: See on 199.
840. edidit: < *edo,* here "give forth, utter."
ore: "manner of speaking" (cf. 124).
841. per: "by," a regular meaning in oaths, where *per* is often separated from its object.
841-842. tibi ... tuos: Brutus addresses Lucretia.
843. Tarquinium ... daturum [esse]: indirect statement after *iuro* (841); *poenas dare* = "to pay the penalty" (an idiom).
profuga ... cum stirpe: "along with (his) exiled family."
844. virtus: sc. *mea.*
845. ad verba: "at (his) words."
sine lumine: with *oculos;* "sightless," i.e., lifeless.
846. concussa ... coma: ablative absolute.
847. fertur in exsequias: "is carried (out) for funeral rites."
animi ... virilis: "manly courage"; genitive of description.
848. secum ... trahit: "she takes along with her" the human reactions to her plight, as if they follow in the procession.
invidiamque: "and ill will (toward the Tarquins)."

849. **inane:** "gaping."
patet: "is visible."
850. **concitat:** here, "summons, brings together."
851. **annua:** "for a year."
consul: "a consul"--actually two consuls were the chief magistrates of the Republic, the form of government which commenced at Rome with the expulsion of the Tarquins.
852. **iura:** "control of the government."
regnis: "rule by a king"; dative.
suprema: "last."

853-856. Weather-sign.

853. **an:** "or."
veris: See on 150.
854. **qua:** "in any way."
versa: perfect participle of *verto* with reflexive force; "having turned itself, having changed directions."
855. **Procne:** See on 629. Ovid apostrophizes Procne in her later manifestation as a swallow.
propera[vi]sse: sc. *te* as subject in indirect statement after *quereris*.
856. **tuo ... frigore:** "the cold you feel"; ablative with *laetus erit* ("will rejoice in").

857-862. February 27. Equirria. Conclusion.

858. **iunctis curribus:** ablative absolute; "(his) chariot having been yoked"; i.e., "having yoked his chariot."
859. **ex vero:** "from fact, truly, rightly."
Equirria: neuter plural; in apposition with *nomen*. The name signifies the main activity of the festival in honor of Mars, "horse races" (*equus* + *currere*).
860. **in Campo ... suo:** i.e., the Campus Martius (see on 366), where the races at the Equirria were usually held.
861. **iure:** "with good reason, deservedly."
Gradive: *Gradivus* is an epithet of Mars.
861-862. **tua tempora ... mensis:** March.
863. **venimus in portum:** See on 3. Ovid frames Book II with the image of his poem as a ship.
libro ... peracto: ablative absolute.